· HARVARD LAW SCHOOL ·

International Program in Taxation

TAXATION OF AGRICULTURAL LAND IN UNDERDEVELOPED ECONOMIES

TO

RUTH

TAXATION OF AGRICULTURAL LAND IN UNDERDEVELOPED ECONOMIES

A SURVEY AND GUIDE TO POLICY

Haskell P. Wald

HARVARD UNIVERSITY PRESS
Cambridge, Massachusetts
1959

Distributed in Great Britain by Oxford University Press, London

Library of Congress Catalog Card Number 58–13549

Printed in the United States of America

PREFACE

Land taxes are very old taxes and are not nearly as important today as revenue producers as they were in many past periods. But rather than reaching the end of their usefulness, they are staging a comeback. Particularly is this true in many underdeveloped economies, where both the needs and opportunities for improving the structure and administration of the land taxes have been increasingly gaining official attention.

Despite this new interest in land taxes, and notwithstanding the still large reliance upon them as a revenue source throughout the world, there has been little systematic study of the subject in recent years. The present volume is an attempt to help revive the study of land taxes by taking stock of their present status and their suitability as instruments of development financing.

This volume is a publication of the Harvard Law School International Program in Taxation. It was undertaken as a direct result of the 1954 Conference on Agricultural Taxation and Economic Development, which pointed out the problems and shortcomings of existing land taxes and underscored the large potential contribution a more effective system of land taxation might make to the financing of economic development in many countries. The Conference was held under the auspices of the Harvard Law School International Program in Taxation, which is part of the School's broad program in International Legal Studies. The Conference included participation by the United Nations, the Food and Agricultural Organization, the International Bank for Reconstruction and Development, the International Monetary Fund, and tax and agricultural experts from the United States and a number of foreign countries. The important contribution to the Conference by Professor Walter W. Heller of the University of Minnesota, Consultant to the Harvard Law School Program, is reflected in the published *Papers and Proceedings of the Confer-*

ence and in this volume, which draws heavily upon the reference materials and working papers of the Conference.

The research for this volume was mostly completed during 1954 and 1955, when I was on the staff of the Harvard Law School Program. Although much information which became available after 1955 is included, there has been no attempt to align all references to land tax methods in particular countries with the most recent legislation and practice. This book is not intended as a compendium of up-to-the-minute information on land taxes in particular countries, but rather as a general survey and evaluation of methods and procedures tried at one time or another in different parts of the world.

The close working relationship between the Harvard Law School Program and the United Nations Secretariat has enabled me to utilize the extensive materials on land taxes in developing countries assembled by the Fiscal and Financial Branch of the United Nations Department of Economic and Social Affairs. I am very grateful to Dr. Henry S. Bloch, Director of the Fiscal and Financial Branch, and to various members of his staff who were so generous with their time and assistance.

As a project of the Harvard Law School Program, this volume was prepared under the direction of the Program's Director, Professor Stanley S. Surrey of the Harvard Law School. I received many helpful suggestions from Professors Surrey and Heller, and also from Joseph N. Froomkin and Herrick K. Lidstone, my former colleagues in the Program.

Oliver S. Oldman, Lecturer in International Tax Law at the Harvard Law School, did a thorough and constructive job of reviewing the entire manuscript and also provided wise counsel and needed encouragement at each stage of the project. Through use of early drafts in his classes for foreign tax officials participating in the Program's taxation curriculum, moreover, he was able to detect weaknesses in my proposals and to direct my attention to source materials that I might otherwise have missed. I am very much in debt also to Jonathan V. Levin, whose critical reading of the manuscript helped me to strengthen the analysis of difficult issues and to make numerous stylistic improvements, and to Professor Philip M. Raup of the University of Minnesota who provided invaluable assistance with respect to the proposals for land tax reform in Part Three of the volume. The index was prepared by Katherine McKinstry. Any errors that may remain, as well as the viewpoints and conclusions, are of course solely the responsibility of the author.

Finally, I wish to thank my family for the heavy sacrifice they made, especially in the period after 1955 when my work on this book was confined to evenings, holidays, and weekends.

H. P. W.

March 1958
West Orange, New Jersey

CONTENTS

INTRODUCTION

How to combat the "vicious circle of poverty" in the world's underdeveloped areas is a problem that is sorely testing the talents of economists today. The many technical assistance missions to underdeveloped countries have had to meet this challenge head on, but numerous others have also been drawn into studying this problem, and various research projects have been organized to promote this work. The result has been an impressive reorientation of economic thinking and research toward fundamental questions of economic growth and toward the specific policy issues that arise as countries seek to hasten their economic progress.

Public finance specialists are in the vanguard of those who have taken positive steps to equip themselves for this new professional responsibility. Finding that neither the lessons of financial experience in the more advanced countries nor many teachings of established doctrine can be applied directly to the vital questions of public finance which today's underdeveloped countries need answered, they have made a start at an essentially fresh approach to their subject at the applied as well as the theoretical level.

Largely through the work of numerous technical assistance missions in the field of public finance and through an extensive program of study and data collection by the United Nations Department of Economic and Social Affairs, there is already evidence of new thinking and accomplishment along several lines. Most notable is the manner in which the principles of public finance are being reinterpreted in a dynamic context. This reinterpretation requires both a harmonizing of tax policy with acceleration of economic growth and an intelligent selection of those revenue instruments which are most appropriate at particular stages of a country's development. Mobilization of domestic savings for productive investment has become a central theme of tax policy planning for economic development, and a search is now in progress for more effective methods of drawing off substantial portions of the increased incomes generated by development programs. Tax incentives – which might encourage desirable economic activities and discourage undesirable ones – also assume enhanced importance in this dynamic framework.

Another facet of the new approach is the extension of public finance to embrace the operations of marketing boards, which are prime producers of revenue in some exporting countries, and of multiple exchange rates, which often yield large income and, besides, have tremendous flexibility as fiscal instruments.

Elsewhere in the realm of public finance we find a reviving interest in the traditional fiscal canons of certainty, convenience of payment, and economy of collection – canons which no country, least of all a poor one, can afford to ignore. More attention is also being given to the necessity of adapting revenue measures to the existing institutional setting, such as the educational level of the population, the accounting practices of the business community, the administrative capabilities of the civil service, and local customs and attitudes. These efforts are often stimulated by the unfortunate inclusion of impractical policy proposals in official recommendations of outside experts.

This new horizon of public finance provides a backdrop for the present study of the taxation of agricultural land. The study seeks to organize the body of available information on agricultural land taxation in underdeveloped countries, to subject the prinicipal methods and tax features to detailed testing against the criteria most relevant to these countries, and to derive a set of practical proposals for land tax reform which could be accommodated to differing country settings and would build the tax into an efficient instrument of development financing. Attention is focused on the problems of land taxation in a developing economy where forced saving through fiscal policy is a basic objective and where incentive considerations and difficult questions of taxpayer equity loom large in the government's thinking. Institutional and administrative considerations also command attention throughout the study and serve to temper, and sometimes overthrow, the strict conclusions of economic reasoning.

The confusing array of existing types of land taxes and the fact that these taxes are so prevalent and so deeply rooted in the fiscal experience of virtually all countries argue the importance of their reappraisal in the light of today's goals of financing economic development. Land taxes are often the only promising means of tapping in the required large amounts the income of the agricultural sector, a weighty consideration in view of the key position which agriculture holds in most underdeveloped countries. A reappraisal would seem to be especially timely, moreover, because of the progress already made in land reform in different parts of the world and the indications in quite a few countries that long-standing institutional and political barriers to land tax changes are beginning to crumble.

· PART ONE ·

A PANORAMIC DESCRIPTION AND INTERPRETATION

I

SYSTEMS OF LAND TAXATION

IN UNDERTAKING a study of agricultural land taxes in underdeveloped countries, one is immediately faced with a troublesome problem of identifying and classifying the specific types of taxes to be investigated. The classification, "land tax," though an old one in public finance literature, has never acquired a precise definition.[1] This is understandable because taxes on the ownership or use of land are certainly among the most adaptable of revenue instruments. They have been accommodated to so wide a variety of agricultural conditions, policy objectives, and local customs, that there seem to be almost as many variants of such taxes as there are countries imposing them.

To restrict the present study to the "traditional land tax" – a term used to distinguish the older type of land taxes, such as "land revenue" in the Indo-Pakistan subcontinent, from their modern counterparts, such as property taxes in the United States and most Latin American countries – would be unduly confining. On the other hand, some taxes having a close family relationship with the traditional land tax can also be appropriately examined in the context of income taxation. In Turkey, India, South Korea, and Ethiopia, for example, agricultural income is exempt from the general income tax on the principle that the land taxes are in lieu of income taxes of the conventional type on agricultural income. The ancient tithe, still collected in many parts of the world, surely has strong claim to membership in both the income tax and

[1] See Karl Brauer, "Land Taxation," in *Encyclopaedia of the Social Sciences*, V, 70–73; also, Henry S. Bloch and Nasser D. Ganjei, "Land Taxes," in *Encyclopaedia Britannica* (1957), XIII, 675–677.

the land tax families. Taxes on marketed produce, such as the "istihlak" in some Middle Eastern countries, pose an analogous problem of classification: although collected in the form of sales taxes, their essential justification often is as substitutes for direct taxes on agricultural land.

In the absence of a ready-made dividing line betwen taxes on agricultural land and other taxes paid by the agricultural sector, the present study adopts a broad definition of land taxes. It encompasses all the diverse types mentioned above: land revenue and land taxes proper, property taxes, so-called land income taxes, tithes, and marketing taxes. Even though this decision as to coverage may seem somewhat arbitrary and needlessly at variance with orthodox systems of classification, it best serves the study's basic objective: to investigate a sufficiently large number of alternative approaches to land taxation in the agricultural sector, so that widely applicable conclusions can be drawn with respect to the most promising avenues of tax reform in this important area of tax policy.

In a real sense, all taxes imposed on the agricultural sector, since they are necessarily paid out of income derived from working the land, can be treated as competing forms of land taxation. If that view were adopted here, an even more motley assortment of taxes would need to be covered, such as capitation taxes on farmers, general income taxes on agricultural income, export duties on agricultural products, profits of government marketing boards, and, conceivably, even sales taxes on commodities purchased by farmers.

Not only does the present inquiry reject so sweeping an interpretation, but it is restrictive in other ways. Certain classes of land, notably forests and mineral properties, commonly receive specialized treatment in the tax law, but this aspect of tax policy will not be covered. Likewise, such exactions as "betterment levies" and user charges for water rights will be given only limited attention.

The design of these early chapters has been determined by the need to build the necessary factual groundwork for the analytical appraisal of the principal types of land taxes in Part Two and for the detailed proposals for land tax reform in Part Three. This first chapter surveys the methods of taxing agricultural land in a large number of underdeveloped countries. In addition to clarifying the selection of taxes, the chapter explains the distinguishing tax features and arranges the taxes into a classification system believed to have considerable expositional and analytical value. The description and interpretation are further developed in Chapters II and III, which examine the dominant conceptual and structural characteristics of land taxes and their revenue importance in different countries.

Proposed Plan of Classification

The protean nature of the land tax is manifest above all in the diversity of the tax base. An assortment of bases has been featured from the very start. The earliest land taxes were assessed either on land area – as, for example, the taxes on "Jugera" in Rome and on "hides" in feudal England – or in proportion to the produce – as in the case of the tithe collected by Eastern sovereigns in ancient times.[2] This initial diversity grew enormously with the passage of time.

The tax base is a convenient and meaningful criterion for classifying the different types of land taxes. Not only is the base a readily observed fact, but it is also a major determinant of the economic character of a tax. The legal definition of the tax base, however, may not always be satisfied in practice; therefore, the plan of classification in this chapter looks more to the practice than to the law.

Close examination of the different bases of land taxes in use in the underdeveloped countries suggests an initial grouping into three major categories, depending on whether the taxes are as-

[2] See C. F. Bastable, *Public Finance* (3rd ed.; London: Macmillan, 1927), pp. 425–426.

sessed according to (1) land area, (2) a rental value concept, or (3) an income concept. In addition, a fourth category, here designated as "special purpose taxes," is sufficiently important to be included in the survey. Various subclassifications are also indicated. When area is used, a separation between (*a*) uniform rate and (*b*) classified rate (or graded) taxes is meaningful. When a rental value concept is the base, a distinction can be made between (*a*) annual value and (*b*) capital value. Finally, when an income concept is used, at least four subdivisions are possible: (*a*) tithe, (*b*) gross yield or gross income, (*c*) net income, and (*d*) marketed produce.

It would of course be unrealistic to expect that each and every land tax can be fitted neatly into this or any other taxonomic arrangement. The taxes have had too anomalous a growth – with little evidence of a process of natural selection leading toward improved forms – to permit clear-cut classification. Moreover, some land taxes combine the characteristics of two or more classes. In the following description, more or less random examples of specific taxes in particular countries are used as illustrations.

Taxes Based on Land Area

Land taxes assessed on the basis of land area provide a logical starting-point for this survey. They are the simplest of the different types in structure and administration and among the first in historical sequence.

Uniform Rate

In its rudest and most elementary form, the land tax is levied at a uniform rate according to the area of each taxpayer's landholdings and without regard to the income-producing capacity of the land. The amount of the assessment is determined by multiplying the tax rate, expressed as a flat amount per acre, hectare, or other unit of land area, by the number of units in each taxable tract.

Unless imposed at a very low rate, this type of tax would necessarily be limited to cultivable land. It would seem to be most suitable either to a situation in which land is plentiful, so that none but highly fertile and easily accessible land is cultivated and that only in a simple manner, or to a situation in which the land subject to taxation is exceptionally homogeneous. Each unit of land taxed would then have about the same value and require approximately equal amounts of labor and capital.

There are only isolated examples today of land taxes which are so free of complexity. In India, in the small state of Travancore, the old land tax was abolished in 1945 and a uniform-rate land tax based on area substituted.[3] The introduction of an area tax in Travancore, however, should not be interpreted as a reversion to a primitive form of taxation, since the new tax is coupled with an income tax on agricultural incomes. The flat rate of 14 annas per acre is truly nominal, being lower than the tax previously imposed on the worst barren land. "Thus the basic tax system, while calling upon all landowners to make a token payment, transfers the burden of the land tax from the downtrodden peasant to the rich landlord through the machinery of the income tax on agricultural incomes. . . The uniform rate cuts through a labyrinth of difficulties engendered by the former distinctions between wet and dry lands, between favorable and unfavorable tenures, between barren and fertile areas, and between cultivated and uncultivated plots."[4] The new tax has yielded about half as much as the old land revenue, but the deficiency has been more than recovered by the tax on agricultural incomes.[5]

[3] See V. R. Pillai, "A Basic Tax on Land (The Travancore Experiment)," *Indian Journal of Agricultural Economics*, vol. V, no. 1 (March 1950), pp. 185–190. Travancore is now part of the United States of Travancore and Cochin.

[4] *Ibid.*, pp. 187–188.

[5] The approach followed in Travancore to reform of the land revenue seems to have the support of several Indian scholars; see the set of papers on taxation of land and agricultural income in the same issue of the *Journal*, pp. 185–226. The crux of the proposal, of course, is the administrative feasibility of an equitable income tax levied upon Indian farmers; see *Report of*

In Paraguay the real estate tax on rural land is assessed strictly according to the number of hectares.[6] The tax rate, while uniform within each rural district, varies among the districts. In setting the rates, the tax director is guided by the average value of property in each district. Districts that are relatively favorably situated and have a good grade of soil are ordinarily assessed at relatively high rates.

An area tax is also applied in Tunisia, but it is restricted to market gardens. The law does not differentiate according to the type of garden crop grown, but only between land under irrigation and nonirrigated land, imposing a substantially higher rate on the former.[7]

Classified Rate

The Paraguayan and Tunisian examples of area taxes represent modest departures from the uniform-rate principle; in the one case the rate is differentiated by districts and in the other by type of irrigation. The departure is far more complete in countries which retain land area as the assessment base but determine the tax liability according to a rate schedule which is expressed per unit of land area but is graduated according to the economic classification of the land. This method provides a crude blending of the simple area approach with a more advanced assessment according to land value or produce.

A practical illustration of a classified rate or graded land tax is found in West Jordan (previously part of Palestine), where agricultural land is divided into sixteen categories depending on fer-

---

the Taxation Enquiry Commission, 1953–54 (Government of India, 1955), vol. III, p. 208. Certain features peculiar to Travancore should be noted, such as the relative homogeneity of the land and of the manner of its cultivation, and the relative preponderance of plantations from which the agricultural income tax is derived.

[6] Joseph P. Crockett, "The Real Estate Tax of Paraguay" (A report to the Minister of Hacienda, Asunción, August 25, 1951, mimeographed).

[7] A. I. Qureshi, "Structure and Taxation of Agriculture in Tunisia," *Papers and Proceedings of the Conference on Agricultural Taxation and Economic Development,* International Program in Taxation, Harvard Law School (Cambridge, 1954), pp. 364–365.

tility and use. The tax rates for the different categories range from 4 fils to 70 fils per donum.[8]

The land tax in Ethiopia and the property tax in the state of Pará, Brazil, also are on an area basis. The rates are differentiated according to the use of the land, but the land is divided into fewer categories in these two countries than in West Jordan. The Ethiopian law classifies land as fertile, semifertile, poor, and unmeasured. The tax rates, which are a composite of the former land tax and the old tithe, range from Eth. $15 to Eth. $50 per gasha (a measure equal to approximately 40 hectares). A surtax for educational purposes is also imposed on the same basis.[9] In Pará, the lowest rate of 15 cruzeiros per hectare is for pastures and the highest rate of 21 cruzeiros is for land growing rosewood.[10]

In principle, allowances for differences in the productive capacity or economic value of the land can be made by adjusting either the tax rate or the value of the tax base. As a practical matter, however, there cannot be as many rate classifications as there are different grades of land. At best, the classified rate area tax can recognize only a few broad economic categories of land, such as might be identified under the most rudimentary system of land classification.

Taxes Based on a Rental Value Concept

The second broad category of land taxes — those assessed according to a rental value concept — has the distinction of conceptual kinship with a celebrated economic doctrine, the Ricard-

[8] The methods of land taxation in the Middle East are described in an unpublished study by Professor A. I. Qureshi, formerly deputy economic advisor to the government of Pakistan. The study, which was made with the aid of a grant from the International Program in Taxation, Harvard Law School, is deposited with the Program.

[9] Nathan Marein, *The Judicial System and the Laws of Ethiopia* (rev. ed., Rotterdam, 1951), pp. 200–207.

[10] Information given in letter (dated January 18, 1955) to the author from Mr. Rubens Gomes de Sousa, Rio de Janeiro, Brazil. In all other states in Brazil, the land tax is assessed on the basis of capital value.

ian theory of rent. As originally conceived, however, the taxes in this group probably were designed as instruments of proportional taxation of landowners' income.

Writing in the early nineteeth century, Ricardo reasoned that rent arises on land because the pressure of population brings different grades of land into cultivation. In the face of equal prices in the market, the better grades yield a greater return to the owners than the poorer grades do. Ricardo maintained that the amount of rent for any given plot is determined by the excess of its yield over the yield on "marginal land," defined as the poorest land in actual cultivation, since the latter produces just enough to cover production costs, including the wages of the cultivator, and leaves nothing for rent. From this theory it follows that a tenant farmer can afford to pay the landlord as much as the full "differential rent" and still retain the ordinary rate of return for his labor and capital.[11]

Ricardo's definition of land rent as "that portion of the produce of the earth which is paid to the landlord for the use of the original and indestructible powers of the soil" seemed to endow land taxation based on rental value with a high moral purpose. Thus, some early proponents of that type of tax rested their case primarily on the propriety of society's taxing away income which arises without any exertion or sacrifice on the part of the recipients.[12] As explained in a later chapter, however, the Ricardian doctrine has lost most of its vogue, and for sound reasons.[13] In a

[11] The concept of differential rent is of course applicable to all factors of production, not simply to land.

[12] Implicit in this attitude is a labor or sacrifice theory of the ethical right to property. According to H. J. Davenport, for example, who was an exponent of that theory: "Nothing . . . which is a natural bounty can rightly have been allowed to serve as a source of individual income, to fall into the category of individual ownership" ("Theoretical Issues in the Single Tax," *American Economic Review*, March 1917, p. 1). So that there should be no misunderstanding of Davenport's position, it should be noted that he would not apply the Ricardian theory to the fertility aspects of agricultural land, but only to "position rents."

[13] See below, Chapter IV, p. 80.

felicitous rebuttal of that doctrine, one writer has observed that "the soil of today owes as much to nurture as to nature." [14]

The simplest interpretation of the rental value concept starts with the proposition that land has economic value for the same reason that any other productive agent has value: it will secure a net return for its owner. In the specific case of agricultural land, rental value is the payment that can be obtained in a competitive market for the opportunity to apply common techniques of agriculture in the cultivation of the land, after taking into account its location and other inherent qualities and whatever additional qualities it contains as a result of past human action.

Under this concept, rental value can be expressed either as a rate of payment for the use of the land during a specified period or as an equivalent capital sum. The former method, which is ordinarily stated as an annual rent, is widely used as the basis of assessment under the older land taxes; whereas capital value is the basis for the more modern property taxes. Various differences exist, however, in theory and practice between these alternative applications of the rental value concept in land taxation.

Annual Rental Value

When rental income is included under a modern income tax, landlords generally are required to report their gross annual receipts from rentals and to deduct therefrom expenses attributable to the rented property. When rental value is the basis of a land tax, however, an entirely different method of assessment is followed.

Only the very large landlords are likely to keep income and expense accounts in underdeveloped countries. An income tax on rental income can be successful even though it is collected from only the largest (and, presumably, the wealthiest) landlords; personal exemptions are likely to exclude most small-scale farmers from income taxation in any case. A land tax, on the other

[14] D. T. Lakdawala, *Justice in Taxation in India* (Popular Book Depot, Bombay, 1946), p. 127.

hand, is usually imposed as a form of mass taxation. It is designed to apply to all landlords, large or small, or at least to most of them. The land tax could not work except possibly in plantation economies, if it were dependent upon taxpayers' accounting records, because the majority of the landlords do not keep adequate records.

It might appear that an easy compromise for many countries would be to base the land tax on actual rents paid by tenants to landlords and provide standard allowances for expenses. In the case of owner-cultivated land, the assessment might be determined with reference to rentals and expenses for similar properties which are cultivated by tenants. Although this is the general method applied in a few countries, it is not as free of administrative difficulties as one might expect.

Experience has shown that a satisfactory system of land classification is a basic initial requirement if going rental rates are to be established on a standardized basis for all the different grades and uses of land in each local area. When rents are not recorded in official registers, there may be many obstacles to ascertaining what rents are actually being paid and to keeping abreast of successive changes in rental rates. But whether recorded or not, the rents actually paid cannot be accepted at face value for tax purposes: for example, the rental agreements may be for varying terms of years, with all sorts of provisions as to security of tenure; or the respective responsibilities of landlords and tenants may be divided in different ways; or the rents may diverge from "true, competitive, normal rents" because they are the outgrowth of a long history of unequal bargaining power between landlord and tenant. Moreover, rents are sometimes paid in kind rather than in cash, and must be converted to a monetary value, unless the tax also is collected in kind. Finally, the absence of an openly competitive and active real estate market in most underdeveloped countries imposes an added limitation on the use of actual rental data for the determination of the tax base. One characteristic of an underdeveloped country is the existence of imperfect markets of all kinds. The land rental market — as well as the market for land sales — is typically one of the most imperfect.

Generally speaking, the better assessment methods in use fall into two groups: (1) those which require the officials to estimate the income-producing capacity of each class of land, following presumably standardized land classification and assessment procedures, and then to separate out the part representing rental value; and (2) those which require the officials to appraise the capital value of the land, either by reference to the prices at which land is being sold or in accordance with established standards of appraisal, and then to compute rental value on the basis of an assumed rate of return. Under both methods, the result is a presumptive assessment, rather than an assessment based on any record of individual experience.

The above methods are often used in combination, as a means of obtaining corroborative evidence. Furthermore, the final assessments are greatly affected by empirical procedures. For example, the assessment officers may take the prior valuation as their starting point and apply essentially arbitrary adjustment factors to allow for, say, a change in the price level or in the revenue needs of the government.

The widespread resort to imputation, or presumptive assessment, in land taxation has also been encouraged by another consideration, which is more a matter of principle than of administrative necessity. This consideration applies to many other types of land taxes, not simply to those employing a rental value concept. It is sometimes claimed that assessments which vary each year in accordance with actual income and expenses, or actual rents, would be inconsistent with the conceptual framework of these taxes, because the intention is to tax "normal" or long-term value and not necessarily the actual value at any particular time. It is significant, for example, that the term, "revenue settlement," referring to the fixing of the land tax liability, connotes a high degree of finality and stability with respect to the assessment. This attitude, of course, has important practical aspects. With the tax assessment stabilized for long periods, the administrative burden is greatly reduced. In addition, the tax can then be treated as a fixed charge on the land, thus occasioning less frequent revision of rental agreements.

Among the underdeveloped countries the leading examples of land tax assessments in accordance with an annual rental value concept are found in South Asia. The "land revenue," as the tax is known in that part of the world, is so variform, however, that it is hard to appreciate that the many variations often embody essentially the same conceptual approach.

In the "permanently settled" areas of India and East Pakistan, which represented approximately 20 per cent of the total assessed area prior to the recent land reform, the amount of the tax was fixed in perpetuity by the Permanent Settlement in 1793.[15] In the province of Bengal, for example, the tax was set at ten-elevenths of the then current net rental receipts of the zamindars, the former tax gatherers who were designated by the British East India Company as proprietors of the lands from which they had been collecting taxes. In Madras, where the permanent settlement was not made until a half-century later, the tax was fixed at two-thirds of the then current rentals.[16] The evidence in various historical accounts suggests that "the revenue liability was fixed in rough and ready fashion without any survey or record of landed

[15] It is of considerable interest to note that the same decade also witnessed the fixing for all time of the land tax in Great Britain; see G. Findlay Shirras, *Science of Public Finance* (3rd ed.; London: Macmillan, 1936), p. 398. The permanent settlement in India was prompted by the desire to secure a stable revenue source and by the East India Company's lack of sufficient knowledge of the indigenous land revenue system. In addition, it was hoped that vesting the zamindars with proprietorship rights in the land and at the same time fixing the revenue demand would give them a strong incentive to expand the area of cultivation and improve the land. See Lakdawala, p. 133. The *Report of the Taxation Enquiry Commission, 1953–54,* includes an excellent summary of the history of the land revenue in India, vol. III, pp. 181–188.

[16] See Phiroze Irani, "Structure and Taxation of Agriculture in India and Pakistan," and A. I. Qureshi, "Method of Assessment of the Land Tax in the Indo-Pakistan Subcontinent," in *Conference on Agricultural Taxation,* pp. 368–411.

rights and interests, or any investigation into the productive capacity of the different classes of soils."[17] The burden of the revenue demand became progressively lighter with the passage of time, owing to a considerable extension of the area under cultivation and the rise in prices. It is estimated that the tax has averaged less than 20 per cent of rentals in recent years in Bengal and Madras.[18] Because of the sharp reduction in the weight of the tax in these areas, the Permanent Settlement has been described as having resulted in "an undeserved gift to the landlords, and an unnecessary burden on others."[19]

With the abolition of the Permanent Settlement and the gradual acquisition by the government of the rent-receiving interests of the zamindars, the land tax due from the tenants in lieu of the previously governing rent is being reassessed on the basis of current rental value. Not the entire resultant increase in land revenue, however, is a net gain to the states, since a portion of the proceeds is being used to compensate the dispossessed intermediaries.

In the "temporarily settled" areas of the Indo-Pakistan subcontinent, there is such a baffling medley of assessment procedures and so much uncertainty as to the meaning of the legislative language defining the tax base, that only a few generalizations are possible.[20] From all appearances, the chief objective is to approximate a tax base that is related, at least in a general way, to net rental value. The revenue demand in these areas is fixed for a period of from twenty to forty years, the exact period being in part a reflection of the time required to resurvey and reassess a

[17] Qureshi, p. 396.
[18] Irani, p. 385.
[19] Lakdawala, p. 134.
[20] Several explanations have been offered for the complexity of the Indian land revenue system: (1) variations in land tenure systems among the provinces; (2) the fact that the system is the result of a gradual evolution from indigenous, local practices; and (3) the fact that it was molded into its present shape "by British officers quite independently of one another to suit local circumstances in different provinces" (*Report of the Indian Taxation Enquiry Committee*, Government of India, Calcutta, 1928, vol. I, p. 41).

given area. Most states grant remissions in bad years and a few states in Pakistan have introduced additional flexibility by providing for limited adjustments in line with price changes.[21]

As a rule, the tax base in the "temporarily settled" areas is not determined individually for each cultivation unit, but only for the most productive unit in an assessment circle or for an area as a whole. The tax for the individual units is then fixed at a percentage of that for the top unit, or at a percentage of the combined assessment, the percentages being determined according to indices of relative productivity derived from cadastral surveys. In areas where the village community is well organized and its leaders exercise considerable authority, the village is taken as the assessment unit and made collectively responsible for payment of the tax; elsewhere, the tax obligation rests directly on individual settlement holders.

The large differences in how the rental value concept is applied in sections of India and Pakistan can be illustrated by a few ready examples.[22] In Punjab a rental value is established for each class of soil in each locality on the basis of the actual cash rents being paid for specified soil types or, if the rents are in grain, the equivalent cash values of these rents. Given the tax rate, expressed as a fraction of rental value, the revenue demand can be computed for each class of soil. The cultivator is then assessed according to the size of his field and the classification of his soil. Under the "sliding-scale system" introduced there in 1935, the revenue demand is automatically reduced when actual prices fall below the commutation prices fixed by the government on the basis of twenty-year averages.

Despite a different legal definition of the tax base in Uttar Pradesh, the basic approach seems to be the same as in Punjab, except that more extensive use seems to be made of recorded cash rentals. The tax base in Madhya Pradesh also is measured by the

[21] See below, p. 53.

[22] These are taken from Irani, pp. 387–389, Qureshi, pp. 397–398, and Lakdawala, pp. 135–136. See also, *Report of the Indian Taxation Enquiry Committee* (1928), I, 44–64.

rentals of the landlords, but there the rentals are fixed by "settlement officers."

In other states, such as Madras, the procedure is to establish the money value of the produce of each field, after painstaking and elaborate land surveys and soil classification work. The net produce is then obtained by deducting the average cost of cultivation, including in the cost the estimated value of the cultivator's own labor, and by introducing allowances for such factors as distance from the market and conditions of the roads. The tax assessment is taken as a percentage of the computed net produce. A variant of this method excludes any allowance for the subsistence of the cultivator.[23]

A Bombay settlement authority has characterized the system followed in that state as "avowedly an empirical one." [24] The essential object of the Bombay method is to analyze existing and former revenue assessments with reference to altered circumstances, such as changes in growing conditions, changes in prices, increase in population, new public improvements (such as roads, railways, and canals), and changes in the prices for which land is sold or let. The ease or difficulty with which past revenue was collected is also considered. After a comprehensive study of these and related factors, the total revenue demand is decided for each village and then distributed over the assessable fields on the basis of their relative values as indicated by the grade of soil, source of water supply, and location.

The land revenue system of Burma has much in common with that of many parts of India. The tax base is "net produce," which is defined as "the balance which remains after the normal cost of cultivation is deducted from the value of the normal gross produce at the normal price." [25] An allowance for the labor of the cultivator and his family is included in "normal cost," since the inten-

[23] When there is no subsistence allowance, the tax base may be closer to a net income than to a rental value concept. (See below, p. 30.)

[24] Quoted in Qureshi, p. 404.

[25] J. S. Furnivall, *An Introduction to the Political Economy of Burma* (Rangoon: Burma Book Club, 1931), p. 250.

tion is to approximate net rental value. According to a noted student of the Burmese system, the tax base tended to exceed economic rent because of the manner in which the cost of cultivation was calculated. In his view, "net produce" as defined in the revenue instructions is a "meaningless abstraction" which neither the settlement officer nor the cultivator understands.[26] The detailed stipulations about how to reckon the wages of the cultivator, for example, or how to allocate joint costs among different crops, are said to be without practical significance, except that they provide "a smoke screen which may protect assessments against rational criticism by the public." [27]

Definitional details regarding the assessment base in Burma have lost their significance in recent years because the burden of the land revenue has been sharply reduced by price inflation. Recent rates, in kwats per acre, have been virtually identical with prewar rates, despite a fourfold rise in the price level. The government's income from land revenue has been completely overshadowed by the large profits of the State Agricultural Marketing Board.

Several illustrations of assessment of agricultural land on the basis of annual rental value are found in other parts of the world. The "rural and urban property tax" in Peru, for example, is levied on a tax base defined as gross income less 10 per cent to cover expenses. On rented land, gross income is the actual rent received annually, whereas on land that is sharecropped, it is the value of the produce paid as rent. In either case, the base would seem to approximate annual rental value. On unrented land, gross income is assumed to equal 3 to 6 per cent of the declared value of the land, the exact rate being determined according to local circumstances.[28]

Since 1949 the land tax in Iran has been assessed on the landlord's share of the annual crops, as estimated by land surveys.

[26] *Ibid.*, p. 255; see also, pp. 214–225.
[27] *Ibid.*, p. 253.
[28] A. J. Aizenstat, "Structure and Taxation of Agriculture in Peru," *Conference on Agricultural Taxation*, p. 332.

During the transition to the new basis some farms continue to pay on the basis of the old cadastral surveys which computed tax liabilities according to estimated gross yield.[29]

Annual rental value is also employed as a tax base in Egypt and Cuba, and it was used extensively in the Dutch East Indies until their independence in 1949. The experience in the Dutch East Indies provides a further illustration of the typically hypothetical character of the tax base whenever it embodies a rental value concept. A detailed account of the "land-rent" in Java indicates that it was intended as a tax on land in its two functions, as a repository of economic value and as an index of social standing within the community. Land valuation, which was done initially by the landowners themselves, took both factors into account. Moreover, allowance was also made for the fact that some plots were considered "sebel," meaning that, in the eyes of the natives, they brought misfortune to the owners.[30]

A prominent example of the use of annual rental value as a tax base among the developed countries is, of course, Great Britain, where the system dates back to 1601. Since 1929, however, agricultural land has not been subject to the "local rates" in Britain. Any land void of buildings is tax free.[31]

Capital Value

Another important class of land taxes which employ a rental value concept includes those assessed on appraised capital value. In the many countries having these taxes, capital value is customarily defined in the law as exchange or market value, that is, as the price at which properties are being sold or can be sold.

[29] *Public Finance Information Papers: Iran* (United Nations, March 1951), pp. 40–41.

[30] See J. W. Meijer Ranneft and W. Huender, *Onderzoek naar de Belastingdruk op de Inlandse Bevolking* ("Research into the Tax Burden of the Native Population," 1926). The above information is taken from a digest prepared for the author by Alida G. Braams.

[31] Arthur Collins, "Occupancy Taxes in Great Britain," *Should the U.S. Adopt the British System of Assessing Realty?* Forum Pamphlet Two (Tax Institute, New York, July 1944).

In a hypothetical case in which the value of land is determined exclusively by economic factors operating in a competitive land market, the capital value of the land is nothing more than the capitalized net annual rental value. The two measures of value, if appropriately defined, are reciprocally related, as principal is to interest. To illustrate: if a plot is estimated to yield a net rental income of 100 per year for an indefinite future period and the going rate of interest on capital is, say 10 per cent, the selling price under theoretically ideal circumstances would be 1,000; with a rate of 5 per cent, it would be 2,000.[32] From the viewpoint of the purchaser of land, who may prefer to look at the interdependence from the other way around, rent is nothing more than the return on his capital investment.

Despite this fundamental interdependence between the bases of the capital value and annual rental value taxes, it is important to classify each tax separately, since there are far-reaching differences between them in actual operation. These differences go much deeper than the inescapable divergence between theory and practice in tax administration, although that is certainly an important consideration.

Common knowledge about assessment practices supports this generalization: if two pieces of land of equal economic value were assessed according to annual rental value in one jurisdiction and according to capital value in another, there is only a remote possibility that the resultant tax bases would be reciprocally related, as they should be under ideal conditions.[33] The description of assessment practices in the preceding section indicates that annual rental value as ordinarily assessed for land

[32] The reader should be cautioned against the pitfall of confusing *net rental income* with the cultivator's *net income.* The latter includes the value of the cultivator's own labor and a return on his productive capital; if he also is the owner of the land, his net income includes net rental income as well. Selling value rests upon a rental not an income concept.

[33] Obviously, this statement is not intended to apply to the case in which rental value is calculated by assuming a rate of return on capital value, or to the opposite case of capital value being computed as a multiple of rental value.

tax purposes is largely a "notional value." The tax base is no less artificial or hypothetical in the typical case of assessment according to capital value. Only a small portion of the taxable landholdings are sold in any assessment period. For those that are sold, there may be doubts whether the selling prices, even in an actively competitive market, can be accepted as true indices of capital value, since the selling prices may be influenced by a host of institutional forces and by market imperfections. To administer the tax properly, the officials must place primary reliance upon land classification procedures and other indirect methods of valuation. The extent to which the assessed value of each tract rests upon "solid evidence" will, of course, depend on what information is available to the officials and on how well they do their work.

Moreover, the concept of rental value that is most appropriate for tax assessment purposes is not necessarily the same as that which is most relevant to the determination of capital value in the market place. Rental value is open to several interpretations: (1) actual rental value at the time of assessment; (2) "normal" value as measured, say, by past experience; or (3) anticipated value in some future period. A further distinction is possible when land is not being put to its optimum use: rental value can be measured with reference to either the expected income in its present use or the potential income in its optimum use.

To the extent that the selling price of land is determined by the economic benefits of proprietorship, rather than by intangible benefits such as the prestige of land ownership, it reflects the discounted value of *anticipated* rental income and not necessarily the capitalized value of *current* rental income. Furthermore, the selling price is likely to be associated more closely with the value of land in its optimum economic use than with its value under *less favorable alternative* uses.[34] In contrast, when annual rental

[34] In some countries of Latin America, where land is a favorite object of speculative investment, the value of land often shows little evidence of being related either to existing or potential yield. The high land prices may be due

value is assessed for land tax purposes, it is likely to be determined with reference to *current* rather than *anticipated* income and with reference to the income of the land in its *present* use even though a different use of the land might be more profitable. In effect, taxing capital value is a means of reaching both current income and wealth, whereas taxing annual value permits reaching only the former. These differences between the two bases can be of paramount importance as regards the economic effects of the respective classes of land taxes.

A striking disparity between the results of the two methods of assessment can be found in the case of idle land, especially when the land borders upon an expanding rural area or is in an agricultural area which is expected to experience rapid economic development. In either of these situations the market value of the land can be expected to exceed the capitalization of current rental value. This will also be true for newly planted orchards or land recently shifted to crops having a long period of gestation. When the land tax is based on capital value, it is common to find that the law includes special provision for such properties just as it does for mineral lands and forests.

Divergences between assessments on capital and annual value may also result from differences in the treatment of improvements on the land. Only a relatively few countries with a capital value tax base follow the much-publicized examples of Australia and New Zealand in exempting improvements and taxing only "site value," which is defined as the value of unimproved land.[35] Capital value assessments ordinarily cover at least a few types of improvements; some countries even include the value of farm animals and equipment as well as the value of structural improve-

to the expectation of continued inflation or to the relatively greater security of land compared to other assets as an investment medium.

[35] The methods of taxing "site value" in these countries are described in Ernest Long, *The Taxation of Land Values* (Institute of Municipal Treasurers and Accountants, Westminster, 1939), pp. 22–28. The Land Valuation Law enacted in Jamaica in 1956 changes the basis of land taxation to the unimproved value of the land (as recommended in the report of the Bloomberg Commission, May 23, 1944).

ments on the land itself.[36] Because it is relatively easy to identify the specific assets to be taxed or left untaxed, the capital value approach lends itself more readily to selectivity in the definition of the tax base than does the annual rental value approach.

When agricultural land is taxed on the basis of capital value, the tax is almost always part of a property or real estate tax applied in both urban and rural areas.[37] This arrangement imparts a different orientation to the taxation of agricultural land than that which exists when an annual rental value basis is used. Because capital value taxes are focused on wealth rather than current income, they are less likely to be viewed as taxes in lieu of income taxes.

The assessment practices appear to be even more lax for capital value taxes than for land taxes based on annual rental value. In many countries that have had land surveys and have prepared cadastres, there is decided vagueness as to what the registered values are intended to measure. Moreover, because of the extended period between land surveys – and because of almost universal inflation after World War II – the cadastral values in use are likely to be obsolete. The land valuations are almost completely void of meaning in areas that have not been surveyed. In some countries, such as Argentina, the cadastral value is determined by capitalizing presumptive income from working the land, but there is no evidence that this method yields a more meaningful valuation.

The assessors presumably are guided by a concept of "normal" or long-term market value; they are therefore inclined to discount any strong upward or downward trends in real estate prices. The number of specially trained assessors in the different

[36] Animal taxes are popular throughout the Middle East as companion measures to land or real property taxes.

[37] The capital value assessment may serve an additional purpose, as in Chile, in that it can be used as a basis for the determination of presumptive agricultural income to be taxed under the individual income tax. In the United Kingdom, on the other hand, the rental value of properties (other than agricultural land) is the basis for presuming income for income tax purposes.

countries is very small, however. Many assessors fail to apply such elementary appraisal tools as simple soil classification schedules and unit value tables; more modern techniques, such as scientific soil mapping and productivity surveys, are extremely rare among the countries having capital value taxes. In fact, only a few of these countries have adopted any official assessment manuals.[38]

In Bolivia, for example, the bulk of the rural land has never been appraised but is taxed on the basis of outmoded and incomplete assessments by owners.[39] The property tax in Nicaragua is conspicuously weak due to the fact that there is no general cadastre and recording of property is voluntary. Collection is based on self-assessment. Local assessment boards cannot assess undeclared property unless they possess documentary proof of ownership.[40] In Chile the real estate office is required by law to reassess about one-sixth of the country each year. With prices advancing rapidly each year, however, the assessed values remain far below actual value most of the time.[41]

Much cruder methods of property valuation are followed in assessing rural than in assessing urban real estate. This is to be expected, since the value of real estate is heavily concentrated in the cities.

Among the underdeveloped countries, property or real estate taxes are found most commonly in Latin America, although a few countries of the Middle East have recently shifted to this type of

[38] One of the first programs undertaken by the Government of Puerto Rico after the election of Governor Marin in 1948 was a complete revaluation of real property. The assessment manual prepared to facilitate this work might serve as a model for other countries. See *Standards for Assessing Real Property,* Public Administration Service (Chicago, 1951) and the companion volume, *Procedures for Real Property Assessment in Puerto Rico* (1953).

[39] *Report of the United Nations Mission of Technical Assistance to Bolivia* (United Nations, 1951), pp. 32–33.

[40] *The Economic Development of Nicaragua,* Report of a Mission Organized by the International Bank for Reconstruction and Development (Johns Hopkins Press, 1953), pp. 370–375.

[41] "Structure and Taxation of Agriculture in Chile," *Conference on Agricultural Taxation,* pp. 343–346.

tax. The land tax in the Philippines also is on capital value, as is the real estate tax introduced in Japan in 1950.

Almost every one of these taxes has unique features. In Paraguay, for example, the value of improvements is included in the tax base in cities and towns, but not in rural areas.[42] In Guatemala, a banking law restricts mortgage loans to a maximum of 50 per cent of the assessed value of property; this provision has helped to limit underassessments, especially in rural areas where the need for borrowing is frequent.[43] Prior to 1954 the law in Chile provided for assessments to be reduced by the amount of any outstanding mortgage debt up to 40 per cent of the assessed value.[44]

Taxes Based on an Income Concept

A third major category of land taxes comprises those which employ an income concept to measure the tax base. The fundamental distinction between these taxes and the preceding group of taxes incorporating a rental value concept can easily be missed. In most cases the distinction is not a matter of outward form, which may be similar for both groups, but rather of below-the-surface characteristics related to how the tax base is defined in the law and assessed in practice. As explained above, the rental value concept, whether expressed as annual value or capital value, is directed essentially toward identifying a special class of income: that which is attributable to the properties of the land – to the quality of the soil, the topography of the field, and the location as related to climate, irrigation, and accessibility to markets. The income concept, on the other hand, is more inclusive. It covers not only the income of the land itself but also the income of other

[42] Crockett, p. 2.

[43] It has been estimated that the assessed values represent about 20 per cent of market value for urban property and about 50 per cent for rural holdings in Guatemala (*The Economic Development of Guatemala,* Report of a Mission Sponsored by the International Bank for Reconstruction and Development, Washington, 1951, p. 268).

[44] "Structure and Taxation of Agriculture in Chile," p. 343.

factors of production, such as the value of the labor of the cultivator and his family and the return on capital invested in improvements on the land and in productive equipment.[45]

Like the rental value concept, the income concept as applied in land taxation is susceptible of different interpretations. The tax base can be measured in terms of either physical production or its monetary equivalent; the base can be either total income or cash income, and either "gross" or "net" (i.e., after deduction of expenses). There may be personal exemptions and other deductions, such as for payments for land obtained under a land reform program. Specific illustrations of these alternative applications of the income concept are given below.

Tithe

The tithe, which is the oldest example of a tax assessed on the basis of gross harvest or gross income, is unusual among fiscal instruments, since it is sanctioned by Mosaic and Islamic law and is still being collected by religious bodies in many parts of the world today. The tithe has been used extensively, however, as a secular tax.

In ancient times the secular tithe often was an expression of the belief that the ruler had a part-proprietorship in the land and that his claim to a share of the produce was by virtue of his ownership rights, not his taxing power. This attitude, which has been applied at one time or another to most of the older land taxes, has persisted to the present time in a few countries, especially in the Middle East, where it stands as a barrier to efforts to recast land taxes along modern principles of taxation.

Some of the earliest applications of the tithe were in conquered provinces, where it afforded a convenient method of collecting tribute. The tithe was universally applied by the early Moslem landlords and was the primary source of support of feudal lords

[45] The tax base would not include income produced outside the agricultural sector, such as income from securities, urban real estate, or trading activities, unless the tax were part of a general income tax and not a land tax.

as well as the church in medieval Europe. There also are many early examples of its being collected by Far Eastern rulers.

Although its name implies a rate of 10 per cent, as specified in Deuteronomy 12:6, the tithe was frequently imposed at substantially higher rates. In ancient Egypt the rulers' share was one-fifth of the gross produce. In the Hindu state in ancient India the share varied between one-twelfth and one-sixth; in later periods in India it was as high as one-fourth or one-third.[46] In the Moslem countries, a rate higher than 10 per cent has generally been the rule. Adherence to the principle of a proportional rate, however, seems always to have been a salient characteristic of the tithe.

Many primitive tax practices originated with the tithe and continue to be associated with the taxes patterned after it. For example, the tithe was often collected by the "farming" method of auctioning off the right to collect it to individuals, called "tax farmers," who gathered the tax from the peasants. It was frequently levied on a village as a unit, and not on individual peasants. Payment in kind was common, especially in primitive agricultural communities. Finally, the tithe was almost unique among land taxes in that it did not depend upon a land survey or a land register. The typical method was to have inspectors visit all farms at harvest time and make on-the-spot assessments. A portion of the harvest was sometimes earmarked to be taken later by the tax collectors.

On the other hand, the tithe has not always been simply a crude tax applied uniformly to the gross harvest as assessed at the end of each crop year. The rate was sometimes differentiated according to the form of land tenure, as in Syria after 1905, or

[46] In early India, "the share of produce due to the ruler was assessed upon a village as a whole and its payment was the joint responsibility of the whole village community. The village headman who represented the community allocated this share among the individual owners with due regard to the condition and quality of the land cultivated by them. . . Whatever was produced was heaped on the floor and the division was made in the presence of the king's officers" (*Report of the Taxation Enquiry Commission, 1953–54,* III, 181).

according to the method of irrigation. An important avenue for differentiation among crops and geographical regions was opened whenever official prices were established for valuing each year's harvest and the tax assessment was based on the officially established valuation.

Many countries in the Middle East did not abandon the old tithe until the twenties and thirties of this century. When they made the change, they often chose to carry over certain features of the tithe into the new taxes imposed in its stead. When the tithe was commuted to a property tax in Syria in 1925, for example, the amount of the tax was fixed in accordance with the returns under the tithe in the preceding four years, and the village, not the individual, was continued as the assessment unit. A later amendment permitted a land survey and assessments based on actual yield when a village could show that continued payment in accordance with the old tithe was too burdensome. The "commutation of tithes" in Palestine in 1928 followed a similar course. The rudimentary property tax in Syria was subsequently replaced by a marketing tax, however, while in Palestine a more refined rural property tax based on rental value was later enacted.

The land tax in Lebanon was collected in the form of a tithe until 1951, when it was abolished and the general income tax was extended to agricultural incomes. The new law provides for presumptive assessment on the basis of the old records of land produce. The assessments remain unchanged for five years, unless output increases or decreases by more than 20 per cent of the assessed income.[47]

The foremost present-day example of the traditional tithe is the Islamic *zakat*, or poor tax. In Saudi Arabia the government collects this tax from all Moslems at a rate of either 5 per cent or 10 per cent of gross income, depending upon the method of

[47] Much of the above information on the experience in Syria, Palestine, and Lebanon, and other countries in the Middle East was supplied by Professor A. I. Qureshi (see above, footnote 8).

irrigation.[48] Up to half of the tax can be distributed by the taxpayer to the poor and deducted from his tax liability. The zakat is imposed by the Moslem authorities as a religious exaction in many other parts of the Middle East.

Gross Yield or Gross Income

Several countries have land taxes based on gross yield or gross income but, unlike the tithe, assessed according to the rated productivity of the land rather than by inspection in the field at harvest time. One example is Morocco, where agricultural land is classified into eight categories, according to productivity, and taxed on the basis of gross output as shown in taxpayers' declarations. There are two tax rates, one for Europeans and the other for natives. Europeans pay the higher rate, in recognition of the greater productivity of their landholdings. Only fruits and vegetables are taxed according to the cash value of production.[49]

The land tax collected by the People's Republic of China is another form of a gross produce tax. This tax has again become the cornerstone of the country's revenue system, as in ancient times. There is no uniformity within the country as to rates and methods of assessment. Tax collections are in kind wherever basic crops such as rice or wheat are grown. Production is assessed in accordance with cadastral records insofar as they are available. This method of presumptive assessment, as opposed to ascertained output at the end of each crop year, serves to exempt from taxation any additional produce resulting from good management or unusually favorable weather conditions. Commercial crops such as tobacco, hemp, and cotton are encouraged by preferential "equivalency rates" between such crops and rice or millet. In many areas progressive rather than proportional rates are in effect and personal exemptions are allowed, usually on a per capita basis.[50]

[48] In the cities the zakat is collected from merchants in the form of a 2½ per cent tax on net worth.

[49] Based on information supplied by Bureau of Economic Affairs, United Nations.

[50] See Joseph N. Froomkin, "Structure and Taxation of Agriculture in China," *Conference on Agricultural Taxation*, pp. 419–420.

The "land income tax" in the Republic of Korea has many of the same features, including an impressive record as a revenue producer. The tax on land producing staple crops is assessed at graduated rates on the basis of the average gross harvest as recorded in the cadastre and used under earlier laws for the determination of the registered rental value of the land. On land producing vegetables and orchard fruits, however, the tax is based on actual net income and the tax rate schedule is graduated according to net income classes.[51] Because of the prevalence of double-cropping, the tax is collected twice a year, during July–August and November–December. No personal exemptions are allowed, but provision is made for exemption from or mitigation of the tax in hardship cases or as an incentive to encourage land reclamation and development. The tax is collected in kind on paddies and dry fields producing staple crops, and in cash on other fields.[52]

The tax on olive trees in Tunisia also falls into the category of gross yield taxes. It is levied on the estimated gross value of the average production of the trees. Trees under twenty years old are not taxed. In the general census olive trees are classified by age groups and average production is determined for each group. These records provide the basis for keeping the tax lists up to date.[53]

Net Income

There are only a few examples of land taxes based on net income, and in each one a presumptive assessment is used. Ordinarily, a country that decides to shift its land tax to a net income basis is prepared to abandon the view that income from agriculture should be taxed differently from other income. It

[51] Agricultural income is excluded from the general income tax.

[52] See Haskell P. Wald, "The Recent Experience of the Republic of Korea with Tax Collections in Kind," *Conference on Agricultural Taxation*, pp. 426–428.

[53] See Qureshi, "Structure and Taxation of Agriculture in Tunisia," pp. 361–362.

will therefore integrate the new tax with a general income tax.

The direct tax in Nigeria can be appropriately classified as a land tax with a net income base. It is assessed on the village community as a collective unit, in accordance with estimates of yield if the village land were cultivated up to a good average standard. The assessment is then apportioned among the members of the community according to local estimates of each individual's taxpaying capacity, as measured by his net income.[54]

In contrast to the practice in the rest of India, Madras assesses its land revenue on the basis of "net produce," a concept closely akin to net income. Net produce is derived by deducting from gross value the cultivation expenses (including the wages of labor).[55]

Not so long ago in Burma the land tax was, in effect, based on presumptive net income rather than on rental value. The tax base did not allow for the cost of family labor, but only for other production costs.

When the income tax legislation requires presumptive assessment of agricultural income – a not uncommon arrangement – the tax on agricultural income might be appropriately described as a "quasi" land tax. The presumptive assessments in these cases are likely to depend upon land valuation surveys and to remain unchanged from one year to the next.

Marketed Produce[56]

Certain taxes on marketed produce are, in reality, a form of land taxation. The clearest example is the *istihlak* (consumption tax) imposed in Iraq in 1931 and in Syria in 1944 to replace the

[54] See J. R. Hicks, D. A. Skelton, and S. Phillipson, *Report of the Commission of Revenue Allocation* (1951).

[55] *Report of the Taxation Enquiry Commission, 1953–54*, III, 186.

[56] Various other revenue-raising measures are similar in their effects to the taxes on marketed produce described in this section. Government marketing boards, fiscal monopolies, export duties on agricultural products, and multiple exchange rate systems are examples; see "Survey of Principal Methods of Taxing Agriculture in Underdeveloped Countries," pp. 296–298. Devices of this type are often used as a means of either supplementing or

former land taxes. The istihlak is an indirect tax levied on produce that is brought to the market for processing or sale to wholesalers, consumers, or exporters. The farmer is not taxed on produce retained for his own use.

The istihlak is applied to livestock and livestock products as well as to crops in Iraq, but not in Syria. It is collected at the time when taxable commodities enter "istihlak centers," which are licensed trading centers. The commodities are valued for tax purposes on the basis of prices certified by local administrative councils.

Under the collection procedure in Iraq, producers sell their products to authorized middlemen who are responsible for paying the tax. These middlemen, who are traders rather than government officials, are subject to elaborate reporting requirements and other controls.[57]

Special Purpose Taxes

This final group of land taxes, being a catchall category, does not lend itself readily to a general description. Perhaps the group's most distinguishing characteristic is that the taxes are designed primarily to serve nonfiscal objectives of an economic, political, or social nature. Their revenue yield may be only an incidental consideration.

For the most part, the types of taxes described below fall outside the main area of concern of this study.[58] The part they play in the fiscal structures of underdeveloped countries should not be overlooked, however. Special purpose land taxes of one type or

---

supplanting land taxation. The profits of the State Agricultural Marketing Board in Burma, for example, represent in part a tax on rice cultivators; as a consequence, the land tax has not been increased for many years. When farmers in Taiwan or Iran are required to sell a portion of their produce to the government at below-market prices, they are in effect being taxed just as if a marketing tax were imposed.

[57] See *Public Finance Information Paper, Iraq* (United Nations, 1951).

[58] However, see the discussion of nonfiscal applications of land taxes in Chapter XI.

another are found almost everywhere, often as integral parts of a country's over-all system of land taxation. Even though their revenue yield may be unimportant, they may be closely tied as policy to the government's development program and broad fiscal objectives.

Taxes on Incremental Value

Many writers, not alone the single-taxers, have stressed the peculiar taxable capacity of increases in land values, on the ground that such increases are often due to the ordinary progress of society and not to any expenditure of capital or any exertion or sacrifice on the part of the owners. In the often quoted words of J. S. Mill, "They [landlords] grow richer, as it were, in their sleep, without working, risking, or economizing." [59]

There are several possible methods of taxing the so-called "unearned increment" in land values: (1) a one-time levy may be imposed on the basis of the increment in land value from a fixed date in the past; (2) past increments in value may be taxed at the time of transfer, possibly at rates which vary according to the class of land and the length of time held; [60] (3) finally, provision may be made for taxing future increments in value at specified intervals.[61]

When increments in value are localized and result from a specific public improvement, such as an irrigation project or a new road, an opportunity exists to impose a special assessment, or "betterment levy." In theory, a special assessment aims to determine the portion of the cost of a public improvement that gives rise to a special as opposed to a general benefit, and to apportion that part of the cost among the property owners in the area where the special benefit is localized. The presence of

[59] *Principles of Political Economy* (Boston, 1848), II, 365.

[60] This method has been followed in many German cities; see Yetta Scheftel, *The Taxation of Land Value* (Boston, 1916), pp. 121–189.

[61] This was attempted in the United Kingdom between 1910 and 1920, with disappointing results; see Long, pp. 15–16.

visible local benefits, of course, makes the taxes more acceptable to the local population.

Special assessments have had their widest application in the United States. In view of the fact that they are specifically designed for financing such development projects as irrigation works, flood-control systems, and certain classes of roads, all of which are extremely important for underdeveloped countries, it is surprising to find that special assessments have not had more general use in these countries. Part of the explanation seems to be that special assessments are an effective and efficient method only when they are planned and executed with great care, and that this administrative requirement may be beyond the capacity of most underdeveloped countries. Until recently, these countries showed little interest in seeking out refined fiscal tools of this type.

Penalty (or Incentive) Taxes

Many land taxes have penalty (or subsidy) features, some of which are present by design and others by accident. In Chile, for example, a penalty tax is imposed on land devoted to growing grapes, with the expressed purpose of encouraging farmers in the Central Valley to shift from grapes to other crops.[62] Whenever a government establishes official prices for valuing crops for tax purposes, as in mainland China and South Korea, it has a ready tool for encouraging the channeling of agricultural output in a desired direction. When property tax rates are progressive, as in Argentina and Brazil, the progression may promote the splitting-up of large landholdings, although ability-to-pay considerations may provide the primary justification for the progression.

Numerous other illustrations of penalty taxes may be given. A recently introduced provision in the Egyptian land tax places a heavy interim tax (five times the normal tax) on lands ultimately scheduled for subdivision under the land reform. It is hoped by

[62] H. K. Lidstone, who recently served as a United Nations tax consultant in Chile, has informed the writer that the penalty tax has not had the desired effect, except on small producers.

the government that the tax will lead the present owners to dispose of part of their holdings, so that official action to subdivide the holdings will not be necessary.[63]

Some countries subject land held by absentee owners or business corporations to extra taxation. Absentee owners in South Australia pay an additional 20 per cent over the regular land tax.[64] Both absentees and land-operating corporations are subject to special taxation in Argentina.

Special taxes are sometimes imposed on unimproved land, with the aim of forcing such land into cultivation or curbing land speculation.[65]

Special Taxes on Certain Natural Resources

There are serious economic and administrative obstacles to taxing forests, mines, and oil and gas resources in the same manner as agricultural land. Forests typically mature slowly and do not regularly bring an annual income to the owner, except in the case of rotation cutting.[66] Minerals and petroleum require special tax treatment because they are wasting assets and are uniquely difficult to appraise. A program of natural resources taxation is a rich area of study which cannot be investigated in the present volume.

Summary and Conclusions

This opening chapter has examined in panoramic fashion the morphology of agricultural land taxation in underdeveloped countries. Certain broad categories of land taxes have been identified according to the key structural characteristic of the

[63] See Philip M. Raup, "Agricultural Taxation and Land Tenure Reform in Underdeveloped Countries," *Conference on Agricultural Taxation*, p. 247.

[64] Shirras, vol. I., p. 401.

[65] See below, pp. 219–221.

[66] A manifestly ill-advised provision with respect to the taxation of forests is found in Chile, where all land which is reforested or is planted in forests for the first time is exempt from taxation for twenty years. This provision would seem to afford the wealthy a ready means of tax avoidance.

taxes — the basis of assessment — and the categories have been described with the aid of illustrations drawn from the experience of many countries.

Because of the hybrid nature of many land taxes and the countless points of difference among them, any plan of classification in this area involves a risk of seeming oversimplified and arbitrary in some of its applications. Even within a single country the methods of land taxation are not always uniform. Large gaps in the available information further complicate the classification problem. Nevertheless, the interrelationships among the principal contrasting forms of land taxes must be understood and the individual taxes fitted into an analytical arrangement before one can proceed with a general analysis of land taxation methods.

An interesting geographical pattern emerges from the preceding survey of systems of land taxation. In the newly settled underdeveloped countries, notably in Latin America, the most common form of land taxation is a property tax based on capital value. By contrast, the countries of South Asia and the Far East, which have not experienced large-scale colonization from Europe, have shown a marked preference for tax bases expressed in terms of annual value. The latter form of assessment has been applied in different ways, however. In India, Pakistan, and Burma, which were administered for many years by the British Colonial Office, the taxes have long been tied to a concept of annual rental value. In the Far East (excluding Japan) a more primitive tax base, gross produce, is still being used. Finally, in the Middle East, the method of taxing land has undergone considerable change in recent years. Some countries in this region have shifted to a capital value basis, after long experience with the tithe system, while others have turned to taxes on marketed produce. Egypt, which taxes rental value, has followed a different course from that of most of its neighbors.

Because this chapter's task of presenting a tidy exposition of an incredibly untidy subject has been so difficult and absorbing, the chapter has not described, except by a few scattered references, the extent to which land taxation is currently in a state of transition in many underdeveloped parts of the world. Each year much new land tax legislation is enacted, while in a number of countries proposed changes are continually in the forefront of legislative debate. Among the chief influences accounting for the active interest in problems of land taxation are the disappointing revenue results of most land taxes during the postwar inflation, the strong pressure to find additional revenue for development financing, the necessity for changing the method of land taxation whenever there is a land reform, and the awakening interest of many governments in overhauling their tax systems in line with modern principles of taxation. These developments provide the central themes of several subsequent chapters.

II

DOMINANT CONCEPTUAL AND STRUCTURAL CHARACTERISTICS

As the second part of the background against which the problems of land taxation in underdeveloped countries should be studied, the present chapter describes five conceptual and structural characteristics which broadly dominate the various types of land taxes catalogued in the preceding chapter: (1) impersonal form, (2) cadastral survey, (3) inflexibility of revenue yield, (4) rigid rate structure, and (5) assessment according to notional values. An analysis of these characteristics will help to round out the earlier description of the fundamental properties of each classification of land taxes. Furthermore, it will provide important additional information about individual taxes in specific economic and institutional settings.

Impersonal (In Rem) Form

One of the salient characteristics of land taxes is that, with but few exceptions, they are cast in an impersonal, or *in rem*, mold. Although this characteristic is to a large extent a reflection of numerous practical considerations, it is also an expression of the ideology behind many land taxes.

A surprising amount of insight into the structure and problems of land taxation can be gained through an understanding of the implications of the *in rem* approach. For example, many governments are inclined to support the impersonal nature of the land tax as a matter of principle, as though any steps toward "personalizing" it would corrupt its essential character. In this attitude one can detect traces of the specious cliché about the land tax being paid out of income from the "original and indestructible properties of the soil," a source to which the justifications of private property allegedly do not attach.

Extensive debate over whether specific types of taxes are properly classified as personal or impersonal serves no real purpose, since the answer has no vital bearing on their relative merits as revenue measures. Both personal and impersonal taxes have a place in a well-designed tax system. It is highly instructive, nevertheless, to indicate the way in which many features of land taxation conform to a consistent pattern of the type ordinarily associated with an impersonal rather than a personal levy.

In the final analysis, the economic distinction between personal and impersonal taxation turns upon whether the amount of the tax is determined with or without reference to the status of the liable taxpayer.[1] The source of the tax payment has no bearing upon the distinction, since in their final incidence all taxes, regardless of their form, are paid out of personal income or wealth. Nor is the object of assessment a valid criterion for this purpose; with the exception of a capitation tax, all taxes are apportioned according to some impersonal magnitude, such as the value of property, income, production, or transactions.

A fundamental reason why most present-day land taxes can be said to be impersonal levies is that, in effect, they are discriminatory taxes; they single out for special taxation a particular source of income or form of wealth. To have land taxes that conform, at least in a general way, to the ability-to-pay principle certainly is viewed as a desirable goal, but that goal is not the guiding principle for these taxes as it is for personal taxes. Instead, land taxes typically derive their primary support from other considerations, such as: (1) the theory that the state has historical

[1] The main legal characteristic of an *in rem* tax is that the tax liability is limited to the assessed property and does not extend to any other assets of the taxpayer.

rights in land;[2] (2) the familiar argument of the single-taxers and others that there is a public equity in land values; (3) the benefit principle; and above all, (4) considerations of fiscal expediency and administrative convenience.[3] To the extent that a land tax has its *raison d'être* in any of these arguments, the economic and personal status of the taxpayer need not enter into the determination of the tax liability.

This is not to say that all discriminatory taxation is impersonal. The test of whether a discriminatory tax is personal or impersonal is the reasonableness of the discrimination from the standpoint of its relation to recognized differences in taxpaying capacity.[4] In particular circumstances differential tax treatment of earned and unearned income, for example, might be justified as being consistent with ability-to-pay considerations and, consequently, it might be an appropriate feature of a plan of personal income taxation. It will be shown in Chapter IV that the land taxes in many countries have unmistakable overtones of this sort of thinking.

Some countries have sought to mitigate or eliminate the discriminatory aspect of their land taxes by exempting land income from other forms of taxation,[5] or by integrating their land taxes with their general income taxes. A few countries have moved in the direction of making their land taxes personal by allowing exemptions for family status or by introducing progressive rates. These rather new developments are especially interesting in the light of the evolution of the land tax.

[2] This theory is sometimes called the "regalia principle."

[3] These and other possible justifications for land taxation are examined in Chapter IV.

[4] The discriminatory aspects of impersonal taxation may also be justified as expressions of sumptuary objectives or national economic or commercial policies. See Allyn A. Young, *Economic Problems New and Old* (Cambridge, Mass., 1927), pp. 108–109.

[5] When the land tax is relatively light, exempting land income from other taxes may result in discrimination in *favor* of land income. The exemption of agricultural income from the general income tax in India appears to have created this kind of discrimination.

In its origins, the land tax was doubtless conceived as a method of personal taxation. In primitive economies, which were agricultural for the most part, land value or produce was the best available measure of the taxpaying capacity of the citizens. The ancient institution of the tithe, the progenitor of an important group of land taxes today, was certainly grounded in ability-to-pay thinking. As the forms of tangible wealth multiplied and intangible property made its appearance on a large scale, the land tax was converted to an essentially impersonal levy. The latest trend toward personalization of the tax is thus completing a cycle.

The impersonal form finds its clearest expression in those land taxes which employ a rental value concept, measured by either annual or capital value. As explained above, the underlying purpose of this concept is to identify the value that can be attributed exclusively to the properties of the land, as distinguished from the value resulting from the cultivator's labor and skill and his use of capital equipment.

Significantly, land taxes, in contrast to most other applications of *in rem* taxation, often include features which are designed, in principle, to promote the equitableness of the tax burden distribution. The use of cadastral surveys, which classify land according to productive capacity, and the inclusion of allowances for such factors as costs of cultivation, methods of irrigation, and distances from markets, are motivated in part by equity considerations, but with this important reservation: the aim is an equitable distribution of the taxes among different *farms*, rather than among different *farmers*. Moreover, the concern is for equity within one segment of the community, the agricultural sector, and not necessarily for equity between that segment and the rest of the community. Even within that sector, however, the degree of equity actually achieved ordinarily is far from complete because of a conspicuous lack of success at the administrative level.

The impersonal character of land taxation may be evidenced in numerous other ways. For example, there is the practice of a "land settlement," which fixes the revenue demand for a considerable period of years. When there is no formal settlement, the tax still is unlikely to be adjusted annually with income or rental value changes. In addition, almost all countries impose the tax at proportional rates rather than at progressive rates which might accord more closely with ability-to-pay considerations. When exemptions are allowed, they are more likely to be explained as measures of expediency — for example, the saving in administrative costs resulting from an exemption of very small farms may more than make up for the revenue loss — than as means of furthering equity.

Another manifestation of the impersonal form is that the tax usually is assessed separately on each plot of land, rather than on each taxpayer's aggregate holding. Furthermore, it is levied at the situs of the property instead of at the domicile of the taxpayer, and the assessment customarily is made without regard to the existence of encumbrances on the land, such as a mortgage.

In one way or another, these practices and provisions of the law are related to the view that the land tax falls on property rather than on persons and, therefore, need not take note of the landowner's position. This view, however, is not acceptable as an application of the concept of taxable capacity, because land cannot have any taxpaying capacity apart from that of its owners. Capacity is a meaningful concept in taxation only when it is measured with respect to persons, not things. The source of income is relevant to other problems in taxation, but not to the problem of measuring taxable capacity, except insofar as the source influences an individual's ability to pay taxes.

Cadastral Survey

Just as the *in rem* doctrine epitomizes the dominant conceptual influences on the structure of most land taxes, the cadastral survey represents the backbone of the system of administration, at least among the better-administered taxes.

The term "cadastre" refers to an official record of the location, size, value, and ownership (or other basis of occupancy) of each tract of land in a specified area. The record normally consists of (1) a set of large-scale maps on which each "survey plot" appears as a recognizable unit; and (2) corresponding registers which contain in tabular form the information needed to describe and identify each plot. In addition, a system of cross-references between the maps and registers is needed.

The early cadastres seem to have been prepared primarily for use in apportioning land taxes, but the modern ones ordinarily serve other important purposes. Because the land registers may embody a system of soil classification, together with detailed information on source of irrigation, method of cultivation, crops grown, and volume of production, they may be invaluable for planning measures for the development of agriculture and for administering a system of land-based credit. Cadastres are likely to be part of the formal record of rights in land recognized by law or valid custom; when so used they are important for securing such rights and facilitating transactions in land. Cadastral surveys are also the essential basis for the planning and execution of desired reforms in the land tenure system and the agrarian structure.[6] In fact, they have an important function with respect to virtually every branch of public service connected with the land.[7]

In most Asian countries either the land revenue settlement departments or the tax collection offices are the custodians of the

[6] The interest of the tax officials in better land survey and title recording systems has sometimes led to significant improvements in the tenure structure, even though there was no such intention originally. Examples where this has happened are given in Philip M. Raup, "Agricultural Taxation and Land Tenure Reform in Underdeveloped Countries," *Papers and Proceedings of the Conference on Agricultural Taxation and Economic Development,* International Program in Taxation, Harvard Law School (Cambridge, 1954), pp. 257–258.

[7] See *Cadastral Surveys and Records of Rights in Land,* Food and Agriculture Organization of the United Nations Agricultural Study No. 18 (Rome, March 1953).

cadastral records and carry responsibility for official registration of property rights and other functions of land administration, as well as for assessment and collection of the land taxes. In Latin American countries, however, the cadastre is usually maintained by property registration departments.

As a minimum a cadastre provides the tax officials with the location and boundaries of all taxable properties and the names and addresses of the liable taxpayers. For that reason alone the cadastre is a virtual necessity for proper administration of a land tax, except when the tax is on marketed product or is collected in the form of an annually assessed tithe.

The information in the cadastre on land productivity and value does not follow any set pattern. Much depends on how the land tax is assessed. Where the tax is based on capital value, the cadastre may not go beyond listing the official appraisal, possibly with the value of land shown separately from that of improvements. If the assessors rely chiefly upon sales information and simple unit value formulae, the cadestre may not record specific information on factors affecting the economic value of each tract. In some rural areas of Latin America the cadastral values are self-assessed by the landowners and are hardly ever verified by the tax officials.[8] Under such conditions the information in the cadastre would be of the most rudimentary sort — and quite unreliable.

Many countries of South Asia, on the other hand, tend toward the opposite extreme as regards both the informational detail in the cadastre and the painstaking care with which the cadastre is

[8] This is true, for example, in much of the rural parts of Bolivia; see *Report of the United Nations Mission of Technical Assistance to Bolivia* (United Nations, New York, 1951), pp. 32–33. In Nicaragua, which has no general cadastre, recording of property is voluntary. Undeclared property cannot be assessed unless the local assessment boards possess documentary proof of ownership, such as a sales contract filed at the local tax office; see *The Economic Development of Nicaragua*, Report of a Mission Organized by the International Bank for Reconstruction and Development (Johns Hopkins Press, 1953), pp. 358–359.

prepared.[9] Apart from a complete description of each field and various findings as to soil characteristics, there may also be data on the potential outturn of crops and on certain production expenses, such as payments of water rates, wages, and cost of transportation to a marketing center.

The cadastral records in Korea, for example, include, besides the survey measurements, topographical characteristics, and ownership data, complete information on the grade of land and the types of crops grown on each field, together with estimates of average production in a five-year base period. The latter estimates were used under earlier laws for the determination of the rated rental value, which is also recorded in the cadastre in terms of physical quantities.

The large investment of money and technical skill that is required in the preparation of a satisfactory cadastral survey is a unique phenomenon in the field of tax administration in underdeveloped countries. It is doubtful that the investment in the administration of any other tax in these countries is nearly so costly as it is for the land tax, although the cost of the cadastre should of course be apportioned between taxation and the other important uses that are served.

The experience of the countries in southern and eastern Asia, however, proves that it is within the capacity of comparatively poor countries to establish and maintain satisfactory cadastral records. The fact that surveying and soil-mapping are so time-consuming has doubtless been a deterrent to some countries, but this is being changed by the growing use of aerial photography to supplement the field work. Air surveys can be enormously economical in time and may also save substantial expense on large cadastral undertakings.[10]

[9] See A. I. Qureshi, "Methods of Assessment of the Land Tax in the Indo-Pakistan Subcontinent," *Conferences on Agricultural Taxation*, pp. 396–411, and J. S. Furnivall, *An Introduction to the Political Economy of Burma* (Rangoon, 1931), pp. 250–255.

[10] See Food and Agriculture Organization, *Cadastral Surveys . . .*, pp. 20–24.

Ostensibly, a heavy investment in cadastral surveys should be conducive to equitable assessment of the land tax. A cadastre has another aspect, however, that may result in flagrant inequities among taxpayers: much of the information in the cadastre is dated and may quickly become out of date, especially in periods of rapid change. Because resurveys are expensive and require technically trained staffs, they are made only at infrequent intervals. Most of the Latin American countries — Chile is a conspicuous exception — do not have any firmly established policy with respect to the frequency of resurveys and tax reassessments. In India and Pakistan the resurvey period is generally between twenty and forty years. Although survey teams are continually at work in these countries, only a small area is covered in any one year. The legal requirement in the Republic of Korea and many other countries is for a new survey every ten years, but that requirement is not always observed in practice. Since reassessment of the land tax must ordinarily await a resurvey, the tax assessments remain unrevised over similarly long intervals, except that most countries permit changes in individual assessments in hardship cases.

Apart from the need for periodic resurveys to check changes in boundaries and land use, there is a continuing requirement for regular recording in the cadastre of topographical changes, such as occur when land is washed away or new land is formed by the diversion of rivers or by other natural or man-made forces. For the particular needs of tax assessment, information on current changes is most essential when the agricultural sector is undergoing rapid change, but that is just when the task of keeping the records up to date is most difficult. It should be noted, however, that an accurate, scientific soil classification survey may be valid for extended periods, which is one reason why that type of survey, as opposed to a mere recording of field boundaries and assessed valuations, is so advantageous for land tax administration.

Inflexibility of Revenue Yield

It is interesting to speculate whether many countries would choose to abandon their present practice of holding the land tax assessment constant over several years and shift to a policy of annual reassessment, if cost were no barrier and there were no administrative obstacles to such a change. Although the goal of revenue flexibility is widely endorsed for most taxes, it is largely alien to land taxes, especially where the *in rem* doctrine has a strong foothold. A tax base that is current from year to year is not considered a requisite if the tax is interpreted solely as a symbol of the historical rights of the state in land, or as a semi-feudal payment to the government in recognition of services rendered, or as an expression of the public equity in land values. A stable tax base, set in accordance with long-run considerations, is generally believed to be more compatible with such reasoning.

Those concerned with ability-to-pay and fiscal policy aspects of the land tax will see a striking paradox in the fact that a country may put considerable effort into apportioning the tax according to some abstract standard of net produce, rental value, or capital value, yet not feel any need for keeping the assessment basis current.

The question of whether built-in stability or flexibility of revenue is the appropriate goal must be reserved for later argument.[11] At this point, it will be sufficient merely to clarify the extent to which the different types of land taxes are characterized by inflexibility of yield and to describe various steps that have been taken to soften such inflexibility.

The notion of a land tax fixed in amount for all time, as under the Permanent Settlement introduced in India in 1793, never gained wide support and is all but dead today. Nevertheless, the yield of most land taxes as they are currently administered is highly inflexible because of the long interval between assessment

[11] See below, pp. 202–205.

or settlement periods. This is not true, of course, of taxes on marketed produce and tithe-like levies, since such taxes vary automatically with changes in production and prices. Nor is it entirely true of those taxes that are collected in kind. The latter technique provides flexibility with respect to price but not production changes. It provides the government with insurance against depreciation of the tax base and tax collections during an inflation. On the other hand, when prices are depressed farmers are given a commensurate tax reduction, since the value of the payment in kind is correspondingly less. Closely similar results are obtained when the assessment base is expressed in physical terms and converted to a monetary equivalent by means of official prices fixed during each season by government regulation. The tax on olive trees in Tunisia operates in this manner.[12]

With these exceptions, land taxes are conspicuously inflexible as revenue producers. Aside from reassessments, which are infrequent, the only other common source of responsiveness to changes in prices and production is granting the taxpayer relief in emergency or hardship situations. Wherever the burden of the land tax on farmers is appreciable, there is a need for provisions for tax remission in the event of serious damage to the crop or of crop failure through no fault of the cultivator. A common form of relief provision is that found in the Republic of Korea: whenever the actual harvest is less than 30 per cent of the registered average harvest, the farmer is excused from payment of the tax.[13] In Burma cultivators may apply for remission if the damage exceeds one-third of the normal full crop; the remission granted is proportioned to the loss of the crop.[14] Tax relief is

[12] See A. I. Qureshi, "Structure and Taxation of Agriculture in Tunisia," *Conference on Agricultural Taxation,* p. 362.

[13] See Haskell P. Wald, "The Recent Experience of the Republic of Korea with Tax Collection in Kind," *Conference on Agricultural Taxation,* p. 427. During the disruptive war years, administrative arrangements were often made for basing the tax on the lower actual harvest, rather than on average yield as required by law. No additional tax was imposed when the average was exceeded.

[14] Furnivall, pp. 221–222.

automatic in almost all countries if land is flooded or its topography is changed by, say, a landslide.

In theory, any desired amount of flexibility in revenue yield might be achieved through appropriate changes in the tax rate; as indicated in the next section, however, most governments are reluctant to change the rate frequently.

An interesting approach to giving the land tax some built-in revenue flexibility on the downside is the "sliding-scale system" introduced in Punjab in 1935 and Sind in 1938. Under this arrangement, which was adopted to avoid a repetition of the severe hardship which fixed tax rates caused for farmers during the sharp price decline after 1930, the maximum revenue rates payable during the currency of a settlement are worked out for each assessment circle on the basis of commutation prices (i.e., averages prices during the previous twenty years). The government is bound not to exceed these rates, provided the general price level of the chief staple crops during the two preceding marketing seasons remains at least as high as the commutation price level, while taxpayers are given the benefit of a proportionate remission of taxes whenever the general price level falls below the commutation level.[15]

Mention should also be made of the unintended flexibility which arises, again only on the downside, when there is laxity in handling delinquencies. This seems to be the main avenue of flexibility for the property taxes in Latin America, where the delinquency problem frequently gets out of hand.[16] Needless to say, this is not a recommended method of providing relief from a fixed tax. In most Latin American countries, where the property

[15] *Report of the Taxation Enquiry Commission,* 1953–54, Government of India (Delhi, 1955), III, 196.

[16] Some illuminating statistics on this point are presented by Joseph P. Crockett in a report on "The Real Estate Tax of Paraguay," (mimeographed, Asuncion, August 25, 1951). A tabulation of more than 15,000 rural parcels showed that 53 per cent was delinquent for more than one year, 34 per cent for more than 6 years, 14 per cent for more than 11 years, and 8 per cent for more than 21 years. Delinquency was much more habitual among large than among small landowners.

tax can hardly be described as onerous, the high delinquency rate simply reflects open tax evasion and weak enforcement.

Statistics can be cited for any number of countries to illustrate the extent to which land tax receipts tend to lag behind the growth in land values and crop production. In India the land revenue of the seven Part A States rose by about 50 per cent from 1938–39 to 1951–52, although the index of wholesale prices of major agricultural commodities, which presumably provides a rough gauge of the trend in land values, advanced by approximately 550 per cent during this period.[17] In Mexico, where economic growth has been rapid in recent years, revised assessments and rate increases accounted for an increase of about 60 per cent in receipts under the land tax between 1943 and 1949. On the other hand, the value of income produced in the agricultural sector rose by 150 per cent during these years and the total national income of Mexico increased by 165 per cent.[18]

Never has revenue inflexibility given governments as much concern as in recent years. Because of world-wide inflation almost all countries have had firsthand experience with the difficulties that arise when tax receipts do not keep pace with the rising costs of government. The problem of inflexibility has also drawn wide attention lately because of the special financial requirements of economic development programs. Nurkse and others have demonstrated convincingly that the twin objectives of development and avoidance of inflation place a heavy premium on taxes which respond readily to an expansion in production and national income. In the early stages of development much of the expansion may be centered in the agricultural sector. A flexible fiscal system that applies to agriculture as well as to other sectors would seem to be the only satisfactory method of assuring that a sufficiently

[17] *Economic Development with Stability,* A Report to the Government of India, by a Mission of the International Monetary Fund (Washington, 1954), p. 61.

[18] The above statistics, which exclude municipal revenue, are from Aron J. Aizenstat, "Structure and Taxation of Agriculture in Mexico," *Conference on Agricultural Taxation,* pp. 312, 320.

large share of any increment in income will be absorbed by taxation and made available for capital formation.[19]

Rigid Rate Structure

The built-in revenue inflexibility of most land taxes is intensified by another prominent characteristic of the taxes: the rigidity of their rate structure. This rigidity is partly an ideological phenomenon, as explained above in connection with the doctrinal argument for a stable tax base and a fixed tax, but it can also be attributed in part to administrative considerations. An invariable tax is easier to administer than one which must be calculated anew each year. A good example of the combined effect of both ideological and administrative factors is found in the countries of South Asia, where the land revenue settlement fixes not only the assessment base but also the tax rate. The practice in the United States of setting the local property tax rate annually in accordance with estimated revenue needs seems to have been eschewed by most of the underdeveloped countries.

The resistance to upward adjustments in tax rates may be explained also by other considerations. As the cadastral values are outdated, the probability is high that the original assessments will become less equitable. This would seem to be true regardless of whether the cadastral values are made obsolete because of inflation or because of agricultural changes incident to economic development; the impact of inflation or development on property values and income is not likely to be spread evenly over the agricultural sector. To raise the tax rate without first equalizing

[19] Ragnar Nurkse, *Problems of Capital Formation in Underdeveloped Countries* (Oxford, 1953), pp. 142–152. With respect to development financing, it is interesting to note that Nurkse credits the traditional land tax in Japan with being the "outstanding instrument of forced saving" during the initial period of the country's development (p. 149). The rather unique experience of Japan with the taxation of agriculture contains pointed lessons for today's underdeveloped countries. See also Norman S. Buchanan and Howard S. Ellis, *Approaches to Economic Development*, The Twentieth Century Fund (New York, 1955), pp. 177–184.

the assessments would therefore result in compounding the inequities inherent in the obsolete assessments. Because of this fact, inflexible assessments and stable tax rates tend to go hand-in-hand. The superficially plausible notion that rate changes can be used to compensate for assessment values which are behind the times is not an acceptable solution in most cases. It is fair to say that, whenever an increase in rates is ruled out simply because it would aggravate existing inequities, there exists an immediate need for reassessment of the tax. Besides, the preference for stable rates may also reflect practical political considerations. In view of the ordinarily large representation of agricultural interests in the national assemblies of the underdeveloped countries, the land tax rate is likely to be a sharply debated political issue. Once an agreement is reached, the legislators may have little desire to see the question soon reopened.

Assessment According to Notional Values

The extensive use of notional or artificial values instead of real or actual values as the basis of assessment is another prominent characteristic of land taxes. Like those already discussed, this feature has an important bearing on the performance of these taxes.

The adjective "notional" is preferable as a description of the typical land tax base to "presumptive," even though the latter is more common in tax literature. Strictly speaking, a presumptive measurement of the tax base is a second choice, to be used only when the base is not susceptible of direct measurement. In the case of most land taxes, the emphasis properly belongs on the hypothetical or fictitious nature of the value taken as the base, rather than on the existence of a presumption that the assessed value is indicative of the actual value. The latter presumption often is unwarranted. Notional values may be required by law or sanctioned by custom, even though the corresponding actual values are already known or can easily be ascertained.

To say that the tax base is a notional value is not necessarily the same as saying that it is unrelated to actual value. When reasonably refined methods of appraisal are followed in a well conceived attempt to obtain a true reflection of real value, the resultant assessments will bear a systematic relationship to real values. The objective of many assessment systems is not so much to measure actual values as it is to distribute the tax load among the individual properties in proportion to their respective actual values.

Much of the explanation of why such general use is made of notional values in land taxation is given in Chapter I, as part of the description of the different bases of assessment. Because it is ordinarily neither feasible nor desirable in the case of assessment according to net annual rental value to base the tax on the actual rents paid by tenants to landlords, heavy reliance must be placed upon appraisal formulae for converting the physical characteristics of the land into corresponding economic values. Many such formulae are tied to a fictional concept of a cultivator of average skill, who employs standard amounts of seed, fertilizer, and other production requisites. The rental value of the land to such a cultivator is then taken as the norm. Some formulae are exceedingly crude, as when land is classified into only a few broad classes – such as dry fields, wet fields, orchards, and so on – and the indicated yield is valued at uniform prices. On the other hand, some other methods in use employ highly refined formulae. They may begin with an estimate of gross income, from which are subtracted standard allowances for costs of production; or they may require rating each field in relation to the rental value of a yardstick farm or some other standard producing unit. The objective of these different approaches, however, is to obtain a reasonably accurate index of relative rental value rather than a realistic estimate of actual value.

A similar situation exists with respect to capital value assessments. Selling prices are not a reliable informational source, since they are so easily influenced by special circumstances surrounding the sale, as well as by short-term market factors. Capitalization of rental income, while limited to rental properties and open to the many weaknesses of rental value data, may be more useful than sales information as a basis for a capital value appraisal. A common approach is to rely upon rule-of-thumb appraisal standards, such as a table of unit values classified by soil types, land use, location, and other factors. If the standards are carefully worked out and skillfully applied, they may give reliable results, but few countries seem to be able to meet these requirements. In the typical case — many examples can be found in the United States as well as in underdeveloped countries — the appraisals are made cursorily, according to haphazard methods, by poorly trained staffs. Standards set forth in the law — such as a requirement for full market value assessments — are openly ignored.

Another reason why the quantitative expression of the tax base often is a figment of the assessors is that empiricism plays a large role in the assessment of many land taxes. Assessors may be guided primarily by the previous appraisal and the record of past taxes, making only rough adjustments for observed changes in the condition of the land and in the uses to which it is being put. Errors in the initial assessment thus stand a good chance of being carried forward from one survey to the next. The assessors may continually put off the day when they will start afresh to reappraise each field in accordance with uniform standards, with the aim of equalizing the assessments.

A historical record of production for each field can be a valuable source of concrete evidence for the determination of the tax base. In Korea and parts of China, where the tax is assessed against the "normal" gross harvest of each field, "normal" is usually interpreted as average production in a base period specified by law. Production records are also used by the settlement authorities in some sections of India, but chiefly in support of the estimate of gross income, which is then adjusted to a net basis.

Three types of land taxes, however, are levied against avowedly real rather than notional values. One is the area tax which is assessed according to the size of each field. A second is the tax on marketed produce, which is assessed according to the value of each load of produce when it is brought to the trading center. When the valuation of produce is according to official rather than actual market prices, however, an element of unreality is introduced into the tax base. Finally, there are the tithe and those taxes patterned after it, which are assessed by inspection teams in the field at each harvest time.

Basing the tax on real values supported by readily observed evidence does not necessarily make it easier to obtain fair and accurate assessments or to control tax evasion. Apart from the area tax, which has a large administrative advantage because of its primitive simplicity, the other two types with bases which can be measured in concrete terms at the time of assessment — marketing taxes and tithe-like levies — require a close check over the activities of large numbers of authorized middlemen in the one case, and over field inspectors in the other. Moreover, once the object of assessment moves into distribution channels, usually within a short time after the assessment, there is no longer any direct evidence to substantiate the valuation. Any subsequent verification must rely upon indirect proof. It is significant that tax evasion is reputed to be a harassing problem in both Iraq and Syria, which tax marketed produce, and that the tithe has a long record of arbitrariness and harshness in administration.

III

REVENUE IMPORTANCE

To complete the descriptive background of this study, this chapter discusses the quantitative importance of land taxes in the revenue systems of the underdeveloped countries. Three facets of the subject are investigated: (1) What proportion of total tax receipts comes from land taxes? (2) What has been the trend in land tax collections in recent years? (3) Do the statistics suggest a significant correlation between the relative revenue importance of land taxes in individual countries and the types of taxes employed?

The available statistical information for answering these questions has serious drawbacks. Revenue tabulations are not always obtainable in sufficient detail to show taxes on agricultural land separately from other tax sources. Countries which tax rural and urban property under the same statute, for example, often do not report separately the collections on each class of property. A special problem exists with respect to the few countries collecting land taxes in kind instead of in cash, since in those cases the reported collections cannot be interpreted correctly without information on how the prices used for valuation purposes compare with market prices. Another difficulty with the statistics is that in some countries the only detailed data on revenues are budget estimates of anticipated receipts rather than reports of actual collections.

It is possible, nevertheless, to assemble reasonably satisfactory estimates for a large sample of countries and arrive at a few generalizations about the relative revenue importance of land taxes and the comparative revenue potential of the different types.

The accompanying table provides estimates of the yield of land taxes expressed as percentages of total tax receipts in a recent fiscal year for twenty-one countries. The type of tax in each country is identified in the table according to the plan of classification described in Chapter I. The estimates of receipts relate to the central governments, where a unitary form of government exists, and to central and state (or provincial) governments combined in the case of federal countries.

The countries are arrayed in the table according to the size of the percentages. Because this array is based on only one year's results, it may not be wholly reliable as an indicator of the relative revenue importance of the land taxes in the different countries. Another limiting factor, of course, is that the table's coverage is restricted by the actual availability of statistics. Some omitted countries (notably, North Viet Nam and Taiwan) are known to obtain relatively high yields from their land taxes.

Relative Revenue Importance

The table lists four countries which were dependent upon land taxes for at least one-fifth of their total tax revenue in the fiscal years shown, seven which were dependent to the extent of at least one-tenth, and thirteen to the extent of at least one-twentieth. In the remaining eight countries, land taxes provided from 1 to 4 per cent of total tax receipts.[1]

Many readers, aware of the dominating importance of the agricultural sector in most underdeveloped countries, may find these estimates of the revenue importance of land taxes surprisingly low. Perhaps they have in mind a situation closer to that which prevailed prior to World War II. On the basis of fragmentary data for 1939, it seems that at least three more countries – Burma, India, and Egypt – would be added to the four shown

[1] Owing to deficient statistics, Paraguay is ranked too high in the table. The estimated yield of the Paraguayan real estate tax is overstated in comparison with the taxes in most other countries because it includes taxes on urban and rural nonfarm property, as well as on agricultural land.

in the table as obtaining 20 per cent or more of their total tax receipts from land taxes.

ESTIMATED YIELD OF LAND TAXES IN SELECTED COUNTRIES EXPRESSED AS PERCENTAGE OF TOTAL TAX RECEIPTS [a]

Country	*Type of Land Tax*	*Fiscal Year* [b]	*Per Cent of Total* [c]
China (Mainland)	Gross produce (in kind)	1953	24
Republic of Korea	Gross produce (in kind)	1954	24
Ethiopia	Area (classified rate)	1953	22
Iraq	Marketed produce	1952	20[d]
Syria	Marketed produce	1951	15[d]
Paraguay	Capital value and area	1948	12
Egypt	Annual rental value	1952	11
India	Annual rental value	1954	9[e]
Panama	Capital value	1951	8
Burma	Annual rental value	1952	5
Costa Rica	Capital value	1950	5
Mexico	Capital value	1947	5[e]
Pakistan	Annual rental value	1952	5[e]
Chile	Capital value	1948	4
Cuba	Annual rental value	1950	4
Iran	Annual rental value	1950	4
Nicaragua	Capital value	1951	3
El Salvador	Capital value	1951	2
Guatemala	Capital value	1949	2
Bolivia	Capital value	1950	1
Brazil	Capital value	1950	1[e]

Compiled from data furnished by the Fiscal and Financial Branch, Bureau of Economic Affairs, United Nations, except estimates for Republic of Korea and China, which were computed from government documents, and for Ethiopia, which were supplied by A. I. Qureshi.

[a] Land taxes are defined to include all taxes (other than general income taxes and death duties) on the ownership or use of agricultural land, and also taxes on marketed produce (other than export duties).

[b] Fiscal years ending in years shown.

[c] Unless otherwise indicated, the totals refer to central government tax receipts (including receipts of fiscal monopolies, but excluding other non-tax revenue).

[d] Estimate is for the *istihlak* (marketing tax) collected in lieu of a land tax.

[e] Percentage applies to combined receipts of central government and states or provinces.

Recent Trends

There is ample evidence that land taxes have lost considerable ground in recent decades as a revenue source. The trend in the absolute amount of collections has probably been upward in almost all cases, but the increases have not been fast enough to keep pace with the growth of receipts from other sources. The failure to keep pace is partly explained by the inelastic character of most land taxes — a consequence of both their built-in inflexibility and rate rigidity, as described in the preceding chapter. This inelasticity is most noticeable in periods of economic growth and inflation, such as occurred during and after World War II. In part, too, it is a result of the appearance of new revenue sources and of the pressure on governments to increase their tax collections as much as possible. When governments have had a choice, they have been inclined to favor a strengthening of income or export taxes, or an extension of indirect taxes, over an increase in land taxes.

The lagging yield did not create grave fiscal problems for those countries which were not heavily dependent on land tax revenues before the war. The relative yield of these taxes in Chile, for example, was 5 per cent in 1940, as against 4 per cent in 1948; in Guatemala the decline was from 3 per cent (1939) to 2 per cent (1949), and in Mexico from 7 per cent (1942) to 5 per cent (1947).[2] On the other hand, India and Pakistan, which obtained one-fifth of their total tax receipts from land revenue in 1939, have been collecting less than 10 per cent from that source in recent years, and have experienced a serious financial squeeze because of that decline. Burma is one of the countries which has had remarkable success in finding a new revenue source — the profits of the State Agricultural Marketing Board — to replace land revenue as the main financial support of the government. As much as two-fifths of Burma's tax revenue came from the land tax before World War II.

[2] The sources of these statistics are the same as those given for the table.

Factors in Relative Revenue Importance

A striking result of the tabulation of relative yields is that none of the five countries at the top of the list has the conventional land tax based on either annual rental value or capital value. China and the Republic of Korea, the two highest countries, rely primarily upon collections in kind – which have the virtue of providing automatic protection against depreciation of the tax revenue – and upon assessments based on gross harvest as recorded in land registers. It should be noted that these countries lead the field by a much wider margin than is indicated in the table, because their in-kind collections are valued at below-market prices.[3] Next highest in order of importance of revenue from land taxes is Ethiopia, which has a primitive area tax with four rate classifications according to land usage. Iraq and Syria, the fourth and fifth countries on the list, tax farm produce at the time it is brought to the market, so that the amounts collected tend to fluctuate with changes in prices and marketings.

The comparatively high revenue effectiveness of the land taxes in China and the Republic of Korea can be measured in another way, by estimating the proportion of the grain harvest taken by the government as tax payments in kind. This proportion is estimated at approximately one-third for China,[4] and at 11 per cent (1953) for the Republic of Korea.[5] Although the available data do not permit many such statistical comparisons among the different countries, it seems certain that those proportions are substantially

[3] An estimate of the extent of understatement of land tax collections is available for the Republic of Korea. If the collections are valued at realistic market prices instead of the low official prices, the share of the land tax in the total was between 40 per cent and 45 per cent in 1954, compared with 24 per cent shown in the table. See Haskell P. Wald, "The Recent Experience of the Republic of Korea with Tax Collections in Kind," *Papers and Proceedings of the Conference on Agricultural Taxation and Economic Development* (Cambridge, 1954), p. 429.

[4] W. W. Rostow, *The Prospects for Communist China* (New York, 1954), p. 324.

[5] Wald, p. 429.

higher than in most other areas. In India, for example, the land revenue represented 1 per cent of the gross value of agricultural output in 1950–51.[6] On the other hand, there are countries, such as Burma, which are able to withdraw an exceptionally high proportion of agricultural income through the use of fiscal methods other than land taxes.

In practically all of the countries, of course, many different taxes are paid directly or indirectly by farmers, so that percentages of the type cited in the preceding paragraph do not in any way measure the relative tax burden on the agricultural sector. Moreover, in China as well as in several other countries, an element of taxation is inherent in the government's practice of requisitioning a portion of the harvest at low official prices.

The comparatively high relative yield of the land tax in Egypt, where rental value is the base, reflects both the level of tax rates and the fact that the tax was reassessed as recently as 1947–49. Few other countries with taxes based on rental value or capital value have as up-to-date assessments.

Many factors have a bearing upon the extent to which particular countries rely upon land taxes. Two logically separable questions are involved in a government's decision as to the amount of revenue it should aim to raise from these taxes: first, how heavy a tax load should be imposed on the agricultural sector? Second, how much should be collected by land taxes and how much by other methods? The answer to the first question depends in part on the proportion of national income originating in the agricultural sector. Generally speaking, this proportion tends to be lower in Latin America than in South Asia and the Far East. It is 18 per cent in Chile and 19 per cent in Mexico, for example, while it approaches 50 per cent in India and China. Some of the Latin American countries, however, have proportions above 40 per cent (e.g., Guatemala and Nicaragua). Agriculture's

[6] *Report of the Taxation Enquiry Commission, 1953–54* (Government of India, 1955), I, 73.

share of income is estimated at 45 per cent for the Middle East.[7] These differences partly explain the ranking in the table.

The proportion of total taxes collected from agriculture also tends to vary with the ratio between per capita income in that sector and in industry. The lower this ratio, the lower the relative taxable capacity of the agricultural sector. The available estimates suggest that this ratio ranges between one-fourth and one-third for the underdeveloped countries,[8] with countries with relatively large agricultural populations and a high proportion of income in the agricultural sector having ratios nearer the lower figure.[9]

Another important factor which influences the ranking in the table is the position of the different countries with respect to the availability of alternative methods of tapping the agricultural sector. Many countries find it more expedient to impose export taxes on agricultural products or to raise revenue through marketing boards or multiple exchange rate systems, than to make extensive use of land taxes. The Latin American countries which export coffee and sugar are in this group, as is Burma, which is a large exporter of rice. The profits of the State Agricultural Marketing Board in Burma account for about two-fifths of the

[7] These estimates are only rough approximations. They are taken from Walter W. Heller, "Survey of Agricultural Taxation and Economic Development," *Conference on Agricultural Taxation*, p. 124, except for the Middle East (E. deVries, "The Balance between Agriculture and Industry in Economic Development," mimeographed, Paper for Fourth Meeting of Technicians of the Central Banks of the American Continent, May 1954, p. 10) and for China. In W. W. Rostow, p. 279, the proportion of gross national product originating in agriculture in China is estimated at 40 per cent. This estimate is based on a more restrictive definition of agricultural production than is commonly used; moreover, it is not corrected for the low controlled prices for agricultural output in China. Adjustment for these factors would probably raise the estimate to between 45 per cent and 50 per cent.

[8] This range is used by H. W. Singer, "The Mechanics of Economic Development," *Indian Economic Review* (August 1952), pp. 1–18.

[9] A greater disparity between per capita incomes in agriculture and industry could be shown if the available statistics permitted a comparison of the per capita excess of income over subsistence requirements in each sector. Such a comparison would provide a better index of taxpaying capacity than the per capita income ratios cited in the text.

government's revenue from all sources. Fiscal monopolies in grain and tobacco also have strong appeal in some countries, sometimes as supplements to land taxes. By contrast, very few underdeveloped countries have been able to offset lagging land tax receipts by heavier income taxation of agriculture.

None of the above factors, however, would seem to be important in accounting for the sharp contrast between the percentages of total revenue provided by the land taxes in China and India. These two countries are not very different as regards the proportion of population in agriculture and the proportion of national income originating in that sector, nor as regards the availability of alternative revenue sources. An explanation of the larger relative yield of the land tax in China than in India probably should stress various political considerations and dissimilarities in the organization of agriculture in each country. It would seem valid, however, to base part of the explanation on the structural differences between their respective land taxes, and to infer from the experience in the two countries that the Chinese type of land tax lends itself more readily to use as a large producer of revenue than does the type of tax found in India.

Conclusions

The estimates of the proportion of total tax receipts derived from land taxes in different underdeveloped countries indicate that these taxes continue to be of large importance as sources of revenue in some parts of the world, but that they have become of comparatively small importance in many other parts.

Although numerous factors influence the extent of a country's reliance upon land taxes, it would seem significant that the countries with the less conventional types of taxes have obtained relatively higher yields from their land taxes in recent years than have countries which have land taxes based on annual rental value or capital value. The above-average revenue performance of the land taxes in China and Korea can probably be attributed in large part to the system of collections in kind. In the past the in-kind system was often linked to inefficient practices of tax collection, but it does have a special advantage in that it prevents depreciation of tax revenues during an inflation. Similarly, the yield of the marketing taxes in Iraq and Syria has been relatively well maintained because these taxes are also protected against revenue depreciation induced by inflation.

These conclusions, however, should not be interpreted as indicating the relative desirability of the different types of land taxes. Revenue-producing capacity is but one of several criteria for the selection of appropriate methods of meeting the financial requirements of government. Furthermore, the full revenue-producing capacities of well administered, carefully designed land taxes that are assessed according to modern land classification procedures remains to be tested in the underdeveloped countries.

· PART TWO ·

MAJOR POLICY GUIDES

IV

WHY LAND TAXATION?

SOME FORM of levy tied to the ownership or use of land is found in ancient, medieval, and modern times and in primitive, semideveloped, and advanced economies. To explain why this type of tax is probably the oldest and most widely used source of governmental revenue, it is necessary to examine the qualifications of land as an object of taxation and of the land tax as a fiscal instrument.

Several reasons for the unrivaled popularity of the land tax have been given in Part One, where the protean nature of the tax and its pliability are highlighted and illustrations are provided of the manner in which it has been accommodated to radically different circumstances. One of the aims of this second part of the study is to shed additional light on the conjuncture of institutional, economic, sociological, and ideological factors which have been responsible for the unique place of land taxation in fiscal history.

There were obvious and compelling reasons for the almost universal selection of land as the principle tax base in early societies. Aside from human resources, land had no rival in importance as a repository of productive wealth and a source of income in these societies. Thus land was by far the most important source of taxpaying ability, and in many communities it was the only one worthy of note. The physical produce of the land could be assessed by the tax collector either in the field at harvest time or when marketed, and the tax collected on the spot. These hard facts, together with other very practical considerations — for example, land is immovable and impossible to conceal, and its owners or occupants are almost always readily identifiable—placed the administration of at least a rudimentary type of land tax within the reach of the most primitive governments.

The felicitous combination of fiscal expediency and strong attractiveness on economic grounds that gave land taxes their original firm foothold in the tax systems of the world persisted in its more or less elementary form for many centuries. Its influence was clearly apparent, for example, in the decision of the American colonies to rely primarily upon property taxation as the mainstay of their tax systems.

With the expansion of commerce and industry, however, the agricultural sectors in many countries underwent large changes which had important implications for tax policy. Agricultural production increasingly became oriented in the direction of local and world markets. This made for more diversified crops, but at the same time for more specialization among individual farmers. Agricultural land became more valuable as the pressure of population growth caused the expansion of both the intensive and extensive margins of cultivation. Barter trading gave way to trading with precious metals and currency. When the Industrial Revolution vastly hastened the growth of nonagricultural industries, wealth in the form of productive equipment became increasingly more important, as did intangible wealth, representing claims on tangible assets. Not alone in today's economically advanced countries, but even in many of the still relatively undeveloped countries, land has lost its commanding position in national wealth and land produce its dominance in national production.

To assess the qualifications of land as a basis of taxation in this new setting, and to select the specific design of land taxation that would be most suitable in a particular country at its present stage of development, it is necessary to consider many complex and subtle problems which never arose in earlier stages of fiscal history. A basic fiscal requirement in today's underdeveloped countries is tax policies consonant with an accelerated tempo of economic growth. One part of this requirement concerns the responsiveness of the tax system to changes in production and income. Another part concerns the appropriateness of the balance in taxation between agriculture and other economic sectors. Both problems must be resolved in an environment in these countries in which the populace, still mindful of the sting of former repressive fiscal measures, has become more conscious than ever before of the goal of equitable taxation.

At the same time there is constant pressure to find new taxes to finance development and maintain economic stability, which means that no revenue source that has proved productive can easily be relinquished unless the revenue loss can be made up elsewhere. Many governments, moreover, continue to be restricted in their choice of tax instruments by practical administrative considerations, including the fact that development programs are already placing a heavy strain on their administrative capabilities.

The plan of Part Two is to re-examine, first, the classical defenses of land as a basis of taxation, and then to analyze in succeeding chapters the equity aspects, economic effects, and administrative features of different methods of land taxation. The criteria for the evaluation of the principal methods include general tax principles that have been reinterpreted to accommodate the special requirements of today's underdeveloped countries.

Alleged Differences Between Land and Other Factors of Production

The literature on land taxation contains a host of arguments in support of special taxes on land — meaning, in most cases, unequal or discriminatory taxes on land — as a matter of principle and apart from considerations of fiscal expediency. The persuasiveness of these arguments hinges upon the existence of pertinent differences between land and other factors of production. Although it cannot be said that these arguments were necessarily important in the initial resort to land taxes, it does seem that they helped in later periods to strengthen the hands of those who favored continued heavy reliance upon the taxes. More significantly, the theories considered below had a discernible effect on the evolution of land taxation in several countries.

The State's Ownership Rights in Land

One alleged difference between land and other productive factors derives from the argument that in some countries the state has historical rights of ownership in land.[1] Without going into the legal and sometimes religious foundations for this claim, or into the historical development of land rights in specific countries, we might assume the existence of such ownership rights and proceed to examine its relevance to present-day tax policy.

Those who put forth this argument may presuppose that ownership makes the state's right to share in land income legally superior to its right to share in other types of income. But that is faulty reasoning, since an ordinary incidence of sovereignty is that the state can tax any income, any property, or any of its subjects in whatever way it chooses. The state always has the power (subject to constitutional limitations) to impose unequal taxation if it chooses. The identical "canons" of taxation – such as fairness, economy, and certainty – are applicable whether land income is appropriated in the name of a state's taxing power or in the name of its ownership rights in land.

If the state owns land, it may equitably claim the share of the produce that is economic rent, provided it acts promptly upon the emergence of economic rent. So long as the state, as a landlord, has no established policy for the appropriation of economic rent, it is possible that occupiers and cultivators of government land will

[1] The reference here is only to legal rights. The argument that the state has an ethical claim to land values is considered in the next section.

proceed on the assumption that appropriation will never take place. If the state suddenly decides to exercise its historical ownership rights, it leaves itself open to the charge of confiscation. The penalty of the state's delay would be visited upon the individuals who happen now to be the actual propiretors, and not upon society as a whole which carries the responsibility for the delay.[2]

The justification for a special tax on land must be sought in existing conditions and not in history. The fact that a state once had an opportunity to appropriate a surplus profit, such as economic rent, without imposing any hardship on its citizenry does not automatically justify subsequent appropriation of that profit. What was originally a surplus, in the sense of income which is not a payment for sacrifices incurred by the recipients, may in the meantime have become a return to a factor of production. Once the values created by the state's failure to act are generally traded, the recipients of the original gains are able to cash them in. The gains are not a surplus to the new owners.

The important conclusion to be derived from this reasoning is that a state which has indisputable ownership rights in land is entitled to tax away *future* increments of economic rent but not necessarily *past* increments; its right to taxing the latter is no different from its comprehensive power to tax income in any form. This principle justifies, for example, the state's appropriating the full economic rent when land is redistributed under a land reform program and the state withholds title to the land from the new tenants. It also justifies the continuance of an existing special tax on economic rent on government-owned land, provided the special tax does not absorb more than the rent; but it does not justify the stepping-up of the tax unless the increase can be defended in terms of the criterion of distributive justice which should guide all tax policies.

[2] See H. J. Davenport, "Theoretical Issues in the Single Tax," *American Economic Review* (March 1917), pp. 6–10.

A Source of "Unearned Increment"

A more general argument in support of the special fitness of land rent as a subject of taxation is that made by J. S. Mill:

> Suppose that there is a kind of income which constantly tends to increase, without any exertion or sacrifice on the part of the owners; those owners constituting a class in the community, whom the natural course of things progressively enriches, consistently, with complete passiveness on their own part. In such a case, it would be no violation of the principles on which private property is grounded, if the state should appropriate this increase of wealth, or part of it, as it arises. This would not properly be taking anything from anybody; it would merely be applying an accession of wealth, created by circumstances, to the benefit of society, instead of allowing it to become an unearned appendage to the riches of a particular class.
>
> Now this is actually the case with rent. The ordinary progress of a society which increases in wealth, is at all times tending to augment the incomes of landlords; to give them both a greater amount and a greater proportion of the wealth of the community, independently of any trouble or outlay incurred by themselves. They grow richer, as it were, in their sleep, without working, risking, or economizing. What claim have they, on the general principles of social justice, to this accession of riches? In what would they have been wronged if society had, from the beginning, reserved a right of taxing the spontaneous increase of rent to the highest amount required by financial exigencies? [3]

The essence of Mill's argument is the following proposition in social ethics: value which arises without any exertion or sacrifice on the part of its owners should not be allowed to become a source of private income. As a means of implementing this proposition, society is enjoined by Mill to use its taxing power to keep unearned gains out of private hands. Many extravagant claims have been made in behalf of this line of reasoning, especially by the single-taxers who see in it the economic answer to the age-old quest for Utopia. Only a small minority goes along with such claims, however; most persons acknowledge that Mill's proposition, while it may have theoretical merit, has little

[3] John Stuart Mill, *Principles of Political Economy* (Boston, 1848), II, 364–365.

practical significance. What are the qualifications needed before the argument can be accepted as a guide to tax policy?

A major qualification, fully appreciated by Mill, has already been treated: like the doctrine about the state's historical rights in land, the present proposition justifies the expropriation of future increases in economic rent but not of increases that have already taken place. As one writer has observed, to "impose on any casual present owner the penalty for a general and institutional blunder appears . . . to be an incredibly unethical position for a school of thinkers whose essential doctrine is one of practical ethics." [4]

A second important qualification is that "unearned increment" tends to be concentrated less in agricultural than in urban land. The landlords who "grow richer in their sleep" are likely to own urban or suburban sites rather than farm land, with the notable exception of instances when the latter unexpectedly proves to be a source of mineral wealth.

In most countries only a small portion of the actual rent on today's farm land represents the value of original properties of the soil. The nutrients necessary for plant growth can be put into the land or taken out of it; that is, land as a source of economic value is not indestructible, but can be depleted or restored. Furthermore, wherever clearing, drainage, road building, or sod-breaking is involved, the "gift of nature" segment of land value is likely to play a relatively minor role. "It is hard to find a situation where some, and in most cases a great deal, of capital has not been invested and incorporated in land that is being farmed." [5] Much of land rent, therefore, is actually a return on the capital invested in maintaining and improving the soil. "Pure rent," wherever it exists, is inextricably mixed with interest on capital investment. Site value is the only clear-cut example of income arising "through the natural course of things."

[4] Davenport, p. 2.

[5] Theodore W. Schultz, *The Economic Organization of Agriculture* (New York, 1953), p. 140.

At the time Mill wrote, he was probably correct in describing land rent as "a kind of income which constantly tends to increase." Insofar as rent on agricultural land is concerned, however, history has not borne him out. Because of advances in techniques of production, use of more capital, and more efficient organization, agricultural land seems to have become less important as a critical limitational factor in economic progress. Economic development operates to relax "the earlier iron grip of the niggardliness of nature." [6] The experience in almost all Western countries seems to support these two generalizations: first, as a community develops, a declining proportion of its aggregate income is claimed by farm products; and, second, the value contributed by land to farm production is not an increasing proportion. Wherever these generalizations hold, the relative economic importance of agricultural land will necessarily decline.[7] Although one must be cautious in predicting that the experience of the developed countries in this regard will be duplicated in today's underdeveloped countries, it is hard to see why the long-term trend in the economic importance of agricultural land in the latter areas will be necessarily upward. Some farm properties will appreciate in relative value in future years — especially in areas newly opened to commercial markets — while other properties will depreciate, with an unpredictable effect on average land values expressed in terms of units of constant purchasing power.

The "unearned increment" principle, therefore — which takes as its premise the distinction between value that is either a gift of nature or the result of the ordinary progress of society, and value that is privately earned — can be employed as an argument in favor of a differential tax on agricultural land only if, first, the tax is forward-looking, so that past increments in value are left untouched, and second, the tax base is confined to "pure economic rent." [8] A tax of this type would probably have a small revenue

[6] *Ibid.*, p. 126.
[7] *Ibid.*, pp. 127–128.
[8] It is sometimes argued that, since unearned increments in land value

potential, however, both in the immediate period and over the long run.[9] This suggests that the most efficient application of the principle may not be in connection with an annually assessed land tax, but rather with a tax on future increments in land value, to be imposed either on the occasion of a transfer of title or an *ad hoc* land revaluation.

Source of Economic Surplus

Having examined the legal and ethical reasons advanced in favor of a differential tax on land, we now turn to some economic arguments. As in the preceding case, these arguments spring from the supposedly unique characteristics of the economic rent of land as a source of income, especially from the view that economic rent is a payment to a *passive* agent of production and is to be distinguished from other returns to agriculture which are payments to *active* agents and therefore necessary to induce economic activity.

A tax on economic rent has been described by Pigou as an ideal tax in its "announcement aspect," for the reason that its amount cannot be altered by any action on the part of the landlord.[10] A tax that hits other agricultural returns, on the other hand, offers an inducement to the taxpayer to adjust his activities in recognition of the tax impact. The long-run effect of these adjustments might be less investment in agriculture and the abandonment of marginal land. A tax on the value of improvements, for example, tends to discourage farmers from making additional investments

---

are only one out of a larger class of such increments, it would be indefensible to appropriate this one class while leaving the others to flourish. In the writer's view this objection is unsound. If one accepts the basic ethical proposition regarding unearned increments, one should not oppose a remedy merely because it fails to do the whole job.

[9] Nothing in the experience with special taxes on land value in the British Dominions — Canada, Australia, and New Zealand — seems to contradict this statement. See, for example, the summary of this experience in Harold M. Groves, *Financing Government* (4th ed.; New York, 1954), pp. 313–314.

[10] A. C. Pigou, *A Study in Public Finance* (3rd ed.; London, 1949), p. 147.

in improvements. In theory, any tax that impinges upon a necessary economic reward tends to have a more deterrent effect on enterprise than an equivalent-yield tax on an economic surplus. It is always possible, however, that any disincentive effects will be outweighed by the "income effect" of taxation, that is, by the economic stimulus which results when taxpayers strive to maintain their customary standard of living despite an increase in their taxes. A tax on an economic surplus has an "income effect," but no disincentive effect.

An integral part of this theoretical reasoning regarding the economic advantages incident to taxes on surpluses is the Ricardian contention that a tax on economic rent is not shifted. The basic theory on this point can be stated simply: if the tax leaves the supply of land unchanged, it will also leave unchanged the volume of products and their prices, thereby closing all possible avenues for tax shifting. By definition, tax shifting, either forward or backward, can only occur through adjustments in market prices.[11]

The Ricardian theory draws a sharp distinction between land and other factors of production, on the basis that land is nonreproducible and therefore fixed in supply, whereas the other factors are not. However, the preceding discussion suggested a basic weakness in this distinction, at least with respect to agricultural land. "Skimming the soil" or exhausting its fertility is certainly equivalent to a reduction in the supply of cultivable land. Only in the case of urban land is the supply a geographical fact and therefore absolutely inelastic.

The basic theoretical proposition regarding the superiority of land as a tax base nevertheless stands: a land tax falling on pure economic rent has the advantage of being a tax on an

[11] The theory assumes that the expenditure of the funds by the government will not affect agricultural production or prices. It also assumes that the landlord always exacts a "rack rent," which is the highest possible rental. If he is not taking full advantage of his competitive position, he may be able to shift part or all of the tax to his tenants, even though the tax does not change his competitive position in any way. The subject of tax shifting is considered in detail in the next chapter, in connection with the equity aspects of a land tax.

economic surplus and thus being neutral from the standpoint of its direct effects on production. In contrast to the ethical argument considered above, the present economic proposition does not require limiting the tax to future increments, since a tax on past increments also is neutral. As in the preceding case, however, the advantage exists only to the extent that the tax is limited to rent differentials associated exclusively with location or "site value." When the tax applies to rental values attributable to soil qualities which are exhaustible, or to improvements on the land, it is no longer a tax on economic surplus.

Applications of the Benefit Principle

The benefit principle of taxation is another reason that has been given for singling out land for differential taxation. Strictly speaking, the conventional definition of a tax as a "compulsory contribution enacted by governments from private individuals without reference to special benefits conferred" leaves no room for the application of the benefit principle in the selection of an appropriate tax base. Paying on a *quid pro quo* basis for what one receives is the rule in the commercial world and the exception in government finance. Most of the government's activities are for the benefit of the whole population, so that the particular benefit to any single taxpayer is indeterminable; moreover, the existence of a broad collective interest in the wide use of governmental services often means that a policy of charging the beneficiaries for what they receive would be incompatible with that interest.

Nevertheless, certain limited applications of the benefit principle are recognized in government finance. Without doubt, the clearest application is found in certain types of administrative charges and fees which are in effect prices rather than taxes. It is customary, also, to recognize a category of "benefit taxes" which fall in a kind of twilight zone between prices and taxes, where the essential elements of taxation are present, but where there is also some relationship between payments to the government and the receipt of specific benefits.[12] A tax on gasoline consumption, for example, is ordinarily considered to be a hybrid levy of that sort, because the amount of tax paid is presumed to bear a reasonably approximate relationship to the benefits derived from the use of public highways.

Many countries impose special charges on land – for example, betterment taxes and payments for water rights – in recognition of specific benefits received. Such special purpose levies, however, are not parts of the land tax proper.

The argument that the benefit principle has a more general application in land taxation should be examined separately for urban and rural land. Two general classes of governmental expenditures benefiting landowners need to be distinguished: (1) direct services provided to landowners and (2) activities serving a broad collective interest but at the same time exerting a favorable influence on land values.[13] In the first class are so-called "land services," such as sewage disposal, garbage collection, fire protection, and maintenance of public water systems and other public utilities. Wherever these services are provided in underdeveloped countries, they are identified almost exclusively with urban rather than rural land. From this standpoint, therefore, the benefit principle would be applicable only to taxes on urban land, and a differential tax on urban real estate might be supported as a substitute for a more complicated system of special fees on a cost-of-service basis. Whether the benefit principle should be applied in this way is debatable, however, since there is a broad public interest as well as a private interest in the provision of "land services." In any event, there would seem to be no basis for a parallel argument in favor of a differential tax on rural land, where such services are usually not provided.

Both rural and urban land might benefit, however, from the second class of government expenditures mentioned above. For

[12] See E. H. Spengler, "The Property Tax as a Benefit Tax," *Property Taxes* (Tax Policy League, New York, 1946), pp. 165–168.

[13] *Ibid.*, p. 170.

example, capital outlays for economic development projects often generate significant increases in land values. In all likelihood, however, the country as a whole and not only the landowners will profit from the outlays. For this reason, the benefit argument, when applied to expenditures of this type, provides an exceedingly slender prop for a general system of land taxation. The most that can be made of the argument is to use it to justify an incremental value tax or, when the increased land values are to a large extent localized, a betterment levy or special assessment. The latter type of levy, if not thwarted by practical considerations, would seem to be especially appropriate for financing irrigation and flood-control projects and also access roads in rural areas.[14]

Conclusions

It has been shown that land taxes owe their origin to a convenient alliance of strategic economic and social considerations, on the one hand, and outright fiscal expediency, on the other. The need for a justification in terms of basic fiscal objectives did not arise until much later, after the taxes had become well established as a source of revenue and governments were able to avail themselves of other opportunities of raising revenues.

Contrary to the claims of the more ardent supporters of land taxes, these taxes do not belong to a fiscal aristocracy; their appropriateness as revenue measures must be tested in each country against the same basic criteria that apply to all other taxes. The preceding inquiry into some common arguments in favor of the unique fitness of land as an object of taxation indicates that the arguments are either misconceived or only of limited applicability today.

Land taxes will continue to have elementary appeal, however, as long as land remains an important source of income and wealth. Moreover, there are undeniable practical advantages in a tax base

[14] See below, pp. 221–223.

that is immovable and easy to detect, and to which is attached so much prestige of ownership in almost all countries. Land taxes also have weighty considerations of expediency in their favor, not the least important of which is expressed by the familiar adage, "an old tax is a good tax." Many governments, too, have a large capital investment in the administrative machinery for their land taxes.

The temptation to be guided primarily by this sort of opportunistic reasoning must be very strong. Yet it would still seem important for all countries to inquire into how closely their land taxes are consistent with the economic and social aims of national policy, and to decide whether these aims might be served more satisfactorily if their present method of land taxation were revised or if needed revenues were raised in other ways.

In the following chapters several types and structural features of land taxes will be analyzed in relation to the key objectives of tax policy in underdeveloped countries.

V

THE VIEWPOINT OF EQUITY

THE SUBJECT of taxpayer equity, or justice in taxation, is one of the most vexing problems of public finance and one of the hardest to place in useful perspective for policy decisions. At bottom, equity is not a concept that is derived by economic analysis, but is a subjective concept with different meanings for different people. Morover, even where there is a consensus on a suitable standard of equity, there may still be disagreement on how closely a particular tax satisfies that standard.

As difficult as it is to find a tax that is equitable to most people's satisfaction, it is infinitely more difficult to find one that is not only equitable but also adequate in yield, economical to administer, desirable in its economic effects, and satisfactory in all other respects. Yet success in the art of making tax policy is never achieved by pursuing only a single goal, such as taxpayer equity, while neglecting others; a determined effort is required to seek out taxes that satisfy, to the maximum extent possible, all the pertinent — and sometimes conflicting — objectives of taxation, with the aim of having the best possible system of taxation in the given situation.

Recognizing the futility of a quest for perfection in the accomplishment of tax policy objectives, policy-makers must be prepared to give ground on some objectives in order to obtain a fuller measure of others. How to assess the probable gains and losses under alternative proposals can present a formidable challenge, however, for these hypothetical results are not measurable quantities. For example, the loss of equity from a manifestly unjust tax feature is not easily weighed in balance against, say, the possible saving in administrative costs by retaining the inequitable provision, or against other possible gains, such as, for example, avoidance of interference with investment incentives or increased effectiveness in controlling inflation. When the policy issues involve comparisons of that sort, the final decisions are likely to be influenced by value judgments that are conditioned by personal biases.

These considerations have profound importance for the present appraisal of land taxes from the viewpoint of equity. In contrast to individual income taxes, which are specifically designed to serve as comparatively refined instruments of equitable taxation, land taxes are much more the product of fiscal expediency or opportunism. This characteristic of the taxes creates a presumption — to be tested later in this study — that even the best land taxes promote only "rough justice" and that the common variety is largely insensitive to basic equity requirements.

In view of the relatively backward state of agriculture in most underdeveloped countries, this further aspect of equity in land taxation is worth stressing at the start of this discussion: the cost of achieving a desirable degree of equity in taxation, if measured in such terms as additional administrative requirements and possible impairment of revenue yield, can be expected to run substantially higher in the agricultural than in the industrial sectors of these countries.

Shifting of Land Taxes

Little purpose would be served by an investigation of the equitableness of different land taxes which did not go beyond the statutory taxpayer. It is necessary to search for the "ultimate taxpayer," defined as the person or persons who incur a real economic loss as a result of the tax. The statutory taxpayer may attempt to recover part or all of his tax liability through adjustment in the terms on which he buys and sells in the market;

moreover, production changes induced by the tax may provide a mechanism for tax shifting.

To trace a tax to its final resting place, however, can be a stubborn assignment. By indicating the conditions that are favorable or unfavorable to tax shifting and the general nature of the results that can be expected when shifting occurs, economic analysis usually can provide the basis for an informed judgment as to the likely distributional pattern of particular land taxes under alternative sets of conditions. In the absence of empirical evidence concerning the actual market effects, however, no amount of theoretical reasoning will provide the final quantitative answers that would be most helpful for policy guidance.

Information on distributional patterns is important apart from what it tells about the degree to which ability-to-pay criteria are served; such information can also contribute to an understanding of the economic effects of taxes. Indeed, to judge the equitableness of a tax independently of its economic effects can be very misleading, since these effects might influence the level and distribution of income and wealth. Because of the close interdependence between equity and economic effects, the following analysis of distributional considerations should be read as a prelude to the more intensive investigation of economic effects in a later chapter; whatever conclusions are drawn with regard to the comparative equitableness of different taxes are subject to qualification and modification in the light of the subsequent investigation.

Basic Theory

The abundant economic literature on the shifting of land taxes is remarkably free of disputation. This does not mean that the writers are in agreement about the application of the theory to specific situations, but merely that no sharp cleavages exist with respect to the basic theory itself. As a point of departure for a search for the ultimate taxpayers, the basic theory and its qualifying assumptions are summarized below in the form of a series of theoretical propositions which are grounded in the general theory of tax shifting and have specific applicability to land taxes.[1] Following the summary the theoretical propositions will be interpreted in the setting of underdeveloped countries and with reference to particular forms of land taxes.

First, according to the basic theory a tax on "pure" economic rent (expressed either as annual or capital value) will always be borne by the landlord. This principle is an application of the commonplace doctrine that a tax on an economic surplus cannot be shifted because it does not affect the cost of production. Under competitive conditions of supply and demand, the market prices of agricultural commodities are determined by the cost of production on marginal land. But marginal land carries no tax when the tax base is restricted to economic rent because, by definition, such land yields no surplus for rent. On better grades of land – intramarginal land – the competitive market rent turns upon their differential yield advantage over marginal land. Therefore, a tax that is no greater than the economic rent will not affect the supply of land under cultivation or induce the owners to shift their production. Without a change in supply – and assuming no induced effects on the demand for agricultural products or on production costs as a result of the expenditure of the tax proceeds — the market prices of agricultural commodities will be unaffected by the tax.

This initial principle has two important corollaries. First, the incidence of a tax on economic rent is independent of whether the land is rented or owner-cultivated, or whether the landlord or tenant is the statutory taxpayer. The market rental which the landlords can exact from their tenants will be the same before the tax as afterwards, because the supply of land to be rented

[1] A standard reference source for the "basic theory" is E. R. A. Seligman, *The Shifting and Incidence of Taxation* (New York, 1910); see the chapter on "Taxes on Agricultural Land," pp. 255–275. The incidence of taxes on agriculture was a favorite subject in classical economic theory; for example, see Alfred Marshall, *Principles of Economics* (8th ed.; London, 1938), pp. 438–439, 794–804.

and the number of tenants seeking land will be unchanged. Should the tenant be the statutory taxpayer, his rental would tend to be reduced by market forces to the extent required to shift the tax to the owner; without such a reduction some land would go unrented, according to the theory, because the tax would leave insufficient income for all the tenants to continue renting.

A second corollary is that landlords cannot shift a tax on economic rent to farm laborers or to suppliers of production requisites such as seed and fertilizer. As just explained, there is no reason why the tax should induce any adjustments in production.

Second, a tax that is greater than the economic rent of land but less than the total rent will be shifted to the extent that the tax discourages landlords from replacing the capital improvements which account for the difference between economic rent and total rent. The total rent may include, in addition to economic rent, the return on (*a*) permanent land improvements, such as clearing and grading; (*b*) the fertility elements in the soil due to the application of fertilizer and adherence to crop rotation and other beneficial practices; and (*c*) other improvements, such as buildings and fences. A tax that exceeds the economic rent impinges on the reward to the labor and capital invested in land improvement. Landlords have some choice with respect to the upkeep of their land; if the after-tax return is not sufficiently attractive, they may decide to allow the land to deteriorate and buildings, fences, and the like to fall into disrepair. The eventual effect may be a smaller amount of produce which may be sold at higher prices. Part of the tax will thus be shifted in the form of increased prices to consumers of agricultural products.

Certain implications of this second proposition might be briefly mentioned. For example, if the tax causes capital to move from the agricultural to the nonagricultural sector, the return on capital will be reduced in the latter sector. This possible result illustrates the common argument that a tax on some forms of capital tends to rest eventually on all forms. But prices of goods produced outside of agriculture will also be reduced, thus serving to compensate for at least part of the price increases on agricultural commodities. The results would be different, however, if total savings were curtailed as a result of the tax, because the over-all level of investment would then decline.

The possibility that shifting to consumers will be limited by international competition also is recognized in the theory. A reduction in domestic production might lead to larger imports, which would tend to hold any tax-induced price rise in check.

Third, a tax in excess of total rent (economic rent plus the return on the landlord's investment in the land) tends to curtail investment in agriculture and to encourage the abandonment of marginal land, with the result that the tax tends to be shifted forward to consumers and backward to laborers and tenants. This proposition would seem to be especially applicable to taxes on land area or gross produce, since the tax base in these cases is far removed from a rental value concept. The greater the tax-induced retirement of land, labor, and capital from agriculture, the larger the reduction in agricultural output and the larger the price rise that can be expected. If, however, the tax on land is part of a general tax on property, there would be no incentive for an exodus of labor and capital from agriculture. The extent of shifting would then depend on how much agricultural land was withdrawn from use and on whether the volume of savings — which determines the volume of investment — was affected by the tax.

Fourth, a tax that is uneven in its initial impact on different classes of land, or that applies to some classes of land and not to others, tends to be spread evenly among all landowners to the extent that land in marginal uses is shifted from heavily taxed to lightly taxed categories. The resultant prices increases for the produce of heavily taxed land will tend to be counterbalanced by price decreases for other produce. If the total tax is less than the economic rent, so that it does not drive any land out of production, there will be no appreciable shifting on balance to consumers; nor will the tax spread to investors outside of agriculture. The main burden of the tax will be seen in the lower net rents of landowners as a group.

These four propositions contain the sum and substance of the basic theory on shifting of land taxes. Like all generalizations in economics, however, they should be applied with caution to specific situations. It should be noted, in particular, that the basic theory outlined above rests on two key assumptions: first, that production is responsive to tax pressures; second, that prices (including rents) are competitively determined in the market place. Because these assumptions are at variance with the facts in most countries, especially those countries in the early stages of economic development, the basic theory should be viewed as only the starting point for the analysis of tax shifting.

A review of the literature indicates that many writers side with Seligman in concluding that "under actual conditions the tax on agricultural land is but rarely shifted to the consumer." [2] Shifting between owners and tenants, on the other hand, is thought to be a more common phenomenon, but one hardly subject to general theoretical principles because of its dependence on institutional arrangements. Other forms of shifting within the agricultural sector, such as backward shifting to farm laborers, are ordinarily dismissed in the literature as having little practical significance.

Each of these aspects of tax shifting is examined below, in relation to conditions that are believed to exist in today's underdeveloped countries. After investigating the circumstances in which taxes on agricultural land might be shifted from the agricultural to other sectors of the economy, the analysis turns to the possibility of tax shifting within the agricultural sector.

[2] Seligman, p. 275. Seligman cites many economists who reach the identical conclusion; for example, see note 1, p. 269. D. T. Lakdawala (*Justice in Taxation in India*, Bombay, 1946) concludes that in India "even an exorbitant tax on land is likely to rest only on the farmer" (p. 128). He argues that the tax will be shared by landlords and tenants.

Intersectoral Tax Shifting

In a competitive free-market economy, the impetus to intersectoral tax shifting will ordinarily be found in a tax-induced reduction in the supply of goods produced for sale outside the sector that is taxed.[3] A lower supply will bring higher prices, thus moving the terms of exchange in favor of the taxed sector and against other sectors. When that occurs, it can be said that the tax is being shifted, at least in part, to the other sectors.

The likelihood of intersectoral shifting of a given tax is dependent, in the first instance, on the place of that tax in the tax system as a whole. Whatever economic forces any single tax sets into motion might be counterbalanced by offsetting influences from other taxes.

All taxes in their initial effects reduce incomes in the sectors in which they are imposed. If the reduction is both universal and equal in size in all sectors, resources everywhere would be subject to equivalent pressure from taxation. Owners of productive resources would then have nothing to gain, tax-wise, by moving resources to other sectors. Only if there is differential taxation, with some sectors being less heavily taxed than others, will the tax system, on balance, exert economic pressure on the allocation of resources.

The following discussion assumes that the introduction of a land tax has no direct effect on other parts of the tax system. Given that assumption, the burden of taxation on resources in the agricultural sector will be increased relative to the burden of previously existing taxes on resources employed elsewhere. The analysis must focus on the consequences of both the added burden itself and the reshuffling of relative tax burdens.

Effect on Costs. Various land tax characteristics can be cited as evidence that the taxes, by adding to the cost of production, might reduce agricultural output. Even when land taxes employ

[3]An absolute reduction is not needed, but only a reduction relative to the supply that would have been offered for sale in the absence of the tax.

a rental value concept, the tax base will almost always reflect the value of some improvements on the land and not simply the site value. Furthermore, the fact that much marginal and even submarginal land in cultivation may be taxed, even when rental value is the tax base, suggests that tax assessments in excess of economic rent are a common practice. As noted in the preceding chapter, pure economic rent is believed to account for only a small part of land value in most countries today. The possibility of a systematic relationship of tax assessments to economic rent would seem to be still more remote when the object of assessment is land area, gross yield, gross income, or marketed produce.

For these reasons, few if any land taxes can claim membership in that fiscal elite which includes taxes paid out of economic surplus. By adding to the cost of production, land taxes usually encroach upon returns to labor and capital in agriculture, thereby creating pressure for resources to leave the industry. If an exodus occurs and, as a result, production declines, the stage will be set for intersectoral tax shifting.

Of course, the preceding argument does not allow for the possibility that the land tax revenues might be spent for purposes that contribute to increases in agricultural production. If the revenues are used in that way, the combined effect of taxing and spending might be a reduction, instead of an increase, in costs of production, and there would then be no impetus to intersectoral shifting.

Conditions of Supply. A necessary link in the chain of reasoning supporting the general case for intersectoral tax shifting is contingent upon the elasticity of supply. If the supply is completely inelastic in the sector that is taxed, a tax-induced increase in costs will not be transmitted outside the sector.

One possible source of supply elasticity in agriculture is that owners of poor land, or of any land that is taxed for more than its economic rent, may decide to abandon it rather than continue cultivation at a remuneration which means a reduced living standard. But is that a likely result? Farmers do not abandon land readily, especially in the older countries where the land may have been in the families' possession for many generations. The typical landowner places a high value on the intangible benefits of land ownership, such as his independence and enhanced social standing in the community, and may be willing, if necessary, to accept smaller monetary rewards than might be obtained elsewhere. Moreover, the fluctuating and uncertain nature of income from agriculture may conceal the impact of the tax for long periods and may encourage farmers to continue working the land in the hope of an eventually favorable turn of the market. An important practical consideration is that the landowners may be tied to their land because of the cost and other hardships of relocating themselves and their families.

The likelihood of a tax-induced abandonment of land would seem to be virtually nonexistent in overpopulated countries, except as a manifestation of widespread ruin and starvation and ruthless tax enforcement. Only the most callous and authoritarian governments in these countries would persist in collecting a tax that was burdensome to the point of forcing farmers to surrender their land, thereby aggravating food shortages and intensifying the unemployment problem. It is usually recognized, however, that a tax in excess of economic rent tends to discourage land reclamation; for this reason, many land tax laws exempt newly reclaimed land from taxation for several years.

The possibility of the land tax leading to an exodus of farm labor does not seem plausible because, as noted below, tax shifting to wages is not a likely result. In any case, an exodus of farm labor, with the amount of land under cultivation remaining unchanged, would have little effect on the supply of agricultural products in overpopulated countries. These countries are characterized by large labor surpluses in agriculture, in such degree that the marginal productivity of farm labor is often claimed to be zero there.

Greater opportunities for the tax to reduce the supply of land under cultivation exist in those underpopulated countries where rapid industrialization is creating attractive employment opportunities outside of agriculture. It is conceivable that some of these countries might even choose to pursue a discriminatory tax policy against agriculture in order to hasten movement to industrial centers. On the other hand, in an underpopulated country in which new regions are still being opened for settlement, the tax may not reduce the total amount of land under cultivation, but may instead put added pressure on farmers to move into richer areas not yet being farmed.

The case of underpopulated countries is interesting from another standpoint. With land plentiful, it is common to find that some cultivable land is being withheld from production for speculative purposes or because of inertia or disinterest on the part of the landowners, even though the land is capable of yielding a profit. A tax on such land would increase the cost of holding it idle, and if the added cost were heavy enough it might force the landowner to bring the land into cultivation or to sell it to someone else for cultivation. Thus, the effect of the tax might be to expand the area of cultivation, to the benefit of the country as a whole. Instead of intersectoral shifting, the tax would rest on the landowners, but at the same time consumers would benefit as more products became available at lower prices.

The elasticity of supply of agricultural production is also a function of the behavior of investment in agriculture. In a situation in which capital flows freely between agriculture and industry, the effect of a land tax, assuming it is a discriminatory tax that is not counterbalanced by equivalent taxes on industry, may be to divert an increased share of the total supply of capital to less heavily taxed branches of industry. The resulting restriction on agricultural production — combined with the stimulus to production outside of agriculture — would shift the terms of exchange in favor of agriculture and lighten its tax load.

It would seem, however, that many of the necessary conditions for a tax-induced diversion of investment are unlikely to prevail in underdeveloped countries, where much of the investment in agriculture is on-the-spot investment in kind, created through the labor of those who work the land. Only an extremely heavy tax would discourage such investment, since most of the labor is firmly attached to the agricultural sector and would otherwise remain idle. Of course, the result might be different for investment in the form of equipment purchased from outside the sector. Inclusion of the value of such equipment in the tax base — or acceptance of its ownership as evidence of taxable capacity in a presumptive assessment — would reduce the advantages to the farmer in making the investment. In certain circumstances, the additional tax might be sufficient to discourage purchases of the equipment.[4]

Finally, the rate of economic development in a country may have an important influence on the elasticity of supply in agriculture. A rapid rate implies a continuous opening of alternative employment opportunities for labor and capital and probably some intersectoral transfers of resources. Supply obviously is more likely to respond to tax pressures in a fluid economy than in a static, sluggish one. The possibility of tax policy being directed toward stimulating intersectoral resource transfers in line with national economic objectives is another illustration of why an appraisal of intersectoral tax shifting should be made within a broad economic context, in which the relationship of taxes to taxpaying capacity is not necessarily the paramount consideration.

The remaining possible sources of supply elasticity in agriculture are unlikely to contribute significantly to intersectoral shifting. The economic variables, other than land and capital, which determine the volume of agricultural production include labor and production requisites such as seed and fertilizer. The inputs of labor and production requisites are established by the prevailing farming practices and, in the case of fertilizer, also by

[4] For example, it has been claimed that the fear of increased taxes has impeded the introduction of technological advances in the rice polishing industry in Southeast Asia. See *Papers and Proceedings of the Conference on Agricultural Taxation and Economic Development* (Cambridge, 1954), pp. 26–27.

the available supply, and are probably not responsive to changes in land taxes.[5] (The possibility that the tax might induce some of the labor force to leave agriculture has already been considered.) Even if these inputs were sensitive to economic pressures generated by taxation, however, it would be impossible to predict whether the tax-induced changes would result in larger or smaller output. On the one hand, the tax would have disincentive effects, because it would absorb part of the return on a farmer's labor and on his investment in production requisites; but on the other hand, the tax would create "income effects" which would provide a positive inducement to the taxpayer to find ways of increasing his income so that he might maintain his living standard despite the tax payment. Economic theory is inconclusive as to which set of opposing effects is likely to be the stronger, although there are compelling practical arguments for concluding that, on balance, the tax would not encourage the taxpayer to slacken his productive efforts.

Effect on Market Prices. The discussion of intersectoral shifting has so far been restricted to the possible effects of a land tax on domestic production. Since any shifting must come through a change in market prices, the relationship between changes in production and changes in market prices must be examined.

For several reasons, elasticity of domestic supply is a necessary but not a sufficient condition for intersectoral tax shifting. In the first place, the effect of reduced domestic output on market prices will be softened if the gap is filled by additional supplies of agricultural products from abroad. International competition is a potent force in the internal markets of many countries, and may set a limit to intersectoral tax shifting. Second, the changes

[5] Even if payment of the tax entailed a strain on the farmers' cash resources, the risk that it would restrict their purchases of fertilizer would seem to be small. The distribution of manufactured fertilizer is often under government control or in the hands of co-operative organizations or traders, with payment not required until harvest time, when any amounts owed for taxes, fertilizer, seed, and loans are withheld from the proceeds of the crop sales.

in the volume of production will not always be transmitted into equivalent changes in the volume of marketings. A substantial portion of the production of food crops, for example, is ordinarily consumed on the farms and never moves out of the agricultural sector. In deciding how much to sell and how much to market, a farmer takes into account not only the requirements of his family, but also the prevailing price in the market and his own needs for cash. One reason why he may need cash is to pay taxes. This suggests that a land tax, by raising the farmer's cash requirements, might actually encourage larger marketings which would depress his selling prices. In effect, the burden of the tax on the farmer would be then compounded: in addition to paying the tax, he would receive a lower price for his produce.

Head taxes have been levied on native populations in parts of Africa with the explicit purpose of bringing more production to the market, and there is certainly a possibility that some land taxes serve that purpose, too.[6] Many countries would, of course, welcome a means of withdrawing additional supplies from the farm, because it would benefit their economic development plans.

A tax-induced incentive to larger farm marketings would not occur, however, when such marketings are themselves the object of taxation, as in some Middle Eastern countries. Instead, the more likely effect of a marketing tax would be to discourage producers from bringing their crops to the marketing centers — an effect that is distinctly favorable to tax shifting. In addition, government regulations may provide an impetus to shifting by requiring the marketing tax to be passed on from middlemen to consumers. Should the marketing tax reduce the net return to producers, it might curtail agricultural production, and not simply marketings, but that possibility would not be any greater under that type of tax than under most other types included in this study.

To sum up, the preceding analysis suggests that the case for

[6] See Walter W. Heller, "The Use of Agricultural Taxation for Incentive Purposes," *Conference on Agricultural Taxation*, p. 224.

any appreciable amount of intersectoral shifting is not persuasive for most forms of land taxes, except possibly in a few under-populated and rapidly developing countries where a heavy, discriminatory tax on agriculture might restrain growth in that sector in favor of more rapid growth elsewhere. Of course, use of the revenues for agricultural development would presumably bring larger production and price decreases instead of the price increases which are the necessary vehicle for tax shifting. But even when the revenues are spent in other ways, agricultural production need not be curtailed by land taxes and prices for agricultural commodities need not rise. The basic obstacle to shifting is the apparent lack of responsiveness of most types of agricultural production to the economic pressures created by taxation.

There are several categories of agricultural income which a land tax might absorb before creating pressures for tax shifting, such as economic rent, rent on permanent improvements, and income that is counterbalanced by the psychic values of land ownership and the hardships of farmers in moving elsewhere. Finally, should production be curtailed by the tax, a price rise for agricultural products might still be largely prevented by an inflow of supplies from abroad or by the failure of the loss of production to reduce the volume of crops marketed. Broadly speaking, the likelihood of the full tax incidence remaining on the agricultural sector would seem to be greatest for taxes based on a rental value concept and least for marketing taxes.

Intrasectoral Tax Shifting

How the tax is distributed among the economic groups *within* the agricultural sector should be of vital concern to most underdeveloped countries because extremely wide disparities in tax-paying capacity are so common there. Except, perhaps, in countries which have recently had a land reform, a small minority — usually large landlords and traders — enjoys a relatively high and sumptuous living standard, while the mass of the agricultural population lives close to the subsistence level.

Relevant Economic Groups. A distinction among the following economic groups within agriculture would seem to be relevant to an analysis of intrasectoral shifting of land taxes: (1) peasant proprietors; (2) large landowners who rent land to tenants, sometimes through a series of intermediary lessees; (3) tenant cultivators; (4) large landowners who operate centrally managed estates and plantations with hired labor; (5) landless laborers who work on estates and plantations or on farms owned by peasant proprietors; (6) communities which are organized on a tribal, village, or family basis and control land under a system of communal tenure; and (7) miscellaneous traders and moneylenders serving the agricultural sector.

Needless to say, these groups vary widely in relative importance from one country to another. Tenancy is generally prevalent in Asia, except where large holdings have been redistributed under recent land reforms. In some parts of the Middle East – Cypress, Egypt, Lebanon, and Turkey — peasant proprietorship seems well established, but in other parts – Iraq and Iran, for example – large landowners still own most of the land, which is cultivated by share tenants. Tenancy is also prevalent in several Latin American countries, although in the Caribbean area, as well as in Ceylon and parts of East Africa, the agrarian structure is dominated by large estates employing paid labor. Systems of communal tenure are the most common form of landholding in the underdeveloped areas of Africa south of the Sahara, and are also found in parts of India, Southeast Asia, and the Middle East, in some of the Caribbean countries, and in the northern and western republics of South America.[7]

Traders and moneylenders play an influential economic role in almost all underdeveloped countries, but are especially important where small-scale farming predominates and where the government's role in agriculture is not large. It is not uncommon

[7] See *Land Reform: Defects of Agrarian Structure as Obstacles to Economic Development,* United Nations, Department of Economic Affairs (New York, 1951), pp. 14–25, 27–33.

to find the trading and moneylending activities in the hands of the large landowners.

The possibilities for intrasectoral shifting depend upon the nature of the economic relationships among the groups living in the agricultural sector. The analytical problem is enormously complicated by the variety and complexity of these relationships and by their dependence upon local institutional, including legal, factors which restrict the free interplay of economic forces. In many respects, therefore, the problem does not lend itself to analysis in terms of general principles of tax shifting, but must instead be examined in the context of a particular tax in a particular country and with the aid of as much inductive evidence as possible.

Shifting through Intrasectoral Price Adjustments (other than rent). A land tax is paid initially either by landowning or tenant groups. The remaining economic groups in agriculture – landless laborers, traders, and moneylenders – may share the tax incidence, however, depending on whether any part of the tax is shifted from the original payers either backward or forward through adjustments in the prices paid or received by landlords or tenants.

One possibility of tax shifting within the agricultural sector is through the operation of government regulations: for example, an increase in the land tax might be accompanied by an upward adjustment in the official prices paid by traders for crops purchased from farmers, or by a lowering of the legal rate of interest charged farmers, or by the subsidized sale of feed, seed, or fertilizer. Such price adjustments, if effective, would be a form of tax shifting, because they would provide partial tax relief to the immediate taxpayers. Although wages paid to farm laborers are sometimes subject to governmental control, it is difficult to conceive a situation in which the government would attempt to enforce tax shifting to laborers, who are usually the lowest income group in agriculture. Rather, the probability is that wage controls will seek to prevent shifting to laborers.

Will backward shifting be induced through the operation of market forces? If the tax does not curtail production — which is the conclusion, with few exceptions, of the preceding diagnosis of opportunities for intersectoral shifting — the basic supply-demand relationships for wages and interest rates will be unchanged. In that event, shifting would not occur automatically through supply-demand adjustments. The problem cannot be dismissed so simply, however, because of likely restraints on the operation of market forces and because tax shifting might assume subtle forms that are not readily detected by the parties who are affected adversely. For example, employers who are required to pay an increased tax might respond by economizing on the housing furnished laborers or on other forms of wage payments in kind. In most countries where wage rates in agriculture are determined largely by custom, where labor is unorganized and lacks political strength, and where workers tend to be immobile, backward shifting of this sort cannot be resisted effectively. A reduction even in money wages is possible in the absence of active competition for workers.

The payment date for most land taxes comes at harvest time. This timing is convenient for the tax collectors but not necessarily for the farmers, who may be placed under pressure to unload their crops when prices tend to be at a seasonal low. If the necessity of raising funds to meet taxes helps to depress the prices obtained by farmers, the tax is made doubly burdensome on them, and at the same time traders' profits will tend to increase. The plight of the farmers will also be aggravated if, because of the timing of the collection of the tax, they are pushed further into debt.

Aside from the price inelasticity of production, perhaps the paramount consideration with respect to the possibilities for tax shifting through price adjustments other than rent is that traders and moneylenders are likely to have the upper hand in dealing with farmers and are able, therefore, to protect themselves against tax shifting, unless, of course, they are prevented from doing so by legislation. Although agricultural laborers are not so favorably situated from a competitive standpoint, but instead are probably in the weakest bargaining position of any group in the economy, the fact that in most countries they earn little if any more than a bare subsistence may be an effective barrier against much of the tax being shifted their way.

If the preceding avenues of tax shifting are without large practical significance, and if the prospect of forward shifting to consumers also is ruled out, then it must be concluded that land taxes imposed on the three landowning groups which do not rent – peasant cultivators, plantation owners, and communal units – are unlikely to be shifted.

Shifting between Landlords and Tenants. Finally, there is the possibility of tax shifting between landlords and their tenants. As a first step two simplifying assumptions can be made: (1) that the amount of land available for rental is unaffected by the tax, and (2) that rents are competitively determined so as to equate the supply of and demand for the available land. Under these assumptions – which underlie the basic theory outlined earlier in the chapter – a land tax imposed initially on owners would not be shifted to tenants because the owners would not be in any more advantageous position to obtain higher rents after the imposition of the tax than before; but a tax imposed initially on tenants would be shifted to owners because marginal tenants would be unwilling to continue renting if landlords did not make allowance for the tax but persisted in collecting rents at the old rates. If some tenants decided to drop out of the rental market rather than pay the tax, competition among landlords for the remaining tenants would force a reduction in rents; otherwise some cultivable land would remain idle. Rental relief granted initially to only part of the tenants would gradually spread to all of them, through the working of competition.

These conclusions do not follow, however, once the assumption as to prevailing rents being competitively determined is lifted. The following review of existing rental practices and regulations in underdeveloped countries will serve to indicate the reasons for the imperfections that characterize most rental markets.[8]

Proportionate produce or share rents are more prevalent in the less developed countries than are rental payments in the form of fixed amounts of produce or fixed sums of money. A common arrangement of long standing in India, for example, as well as in Indonesia, the Philippines, and Thailand, is equal sharing of the crop between tenant and landlord, with each party being responsible for providing certain production requisites. Share rents vary from one-sixth to one-half the crop in Ceylon, and they vary over a similarly wide range in the countries of the Middle East. The landlord's share tends to be substantially higher for irrigated crops, provided the landlord supplies the water, than for dry crops. In general, share rents are lowest in those Latin American countries where land is relatively plentiful and labor scarce.

Fixed produce rents also exist in some parts of India, and until recently they were the customary arrangement in Burma. Cash rents are the commonest form in Egypt, but in most other underdeveloped countries cash rents are restricted to special crops, such as sugar cane in India.

Finally, there are many instances of labor rents. In several Latin American countries, for example, laborers on estates receive a small piece of land from the estate owners, in return for which they work without pay on the owners' land for a specified number of days per week.

Superimposed upon this array of rental arrangements are government rent controls in many countries. An increasing number of countries have adopted legislation aimed at enforcing ceilings on agricultural land rents in recent years.[9] Ceilings introduced in some states in India, for example, vary between one-third and one-fifth of the produce or its value. Recent legislation in Taiwan fixes general ceilings of 37.5 per cent for all leaseholds on private

[8] See *Land Reform,* pp. 15–17.

[9] See *Progress in Land Reform,* United Nations, Department of Economic Affairs (New York, 1954), pp. 139–147.

land and 25 per cent on government-owned land. The ceilings in Taiwan apply to the standard yield, as established for each grade and category of land by official committees, and the rent is expressed and paid in real terms instead of in cash. Progress in bringing rents under government control has been slowest in Latin America.

Wherever rental rates are determined by well-established local custom or by law, rather than by competitive bidding in an active rental market, they will respond slowly, if at all, to changes in land taxes. An additional source of rental inflexibility is present when land is under long-term leases. It should be recognized, however, that the adjustments to tax pressures need not always take the form of a change in the landlord's stated share or in the actual rental payment; adjustments may also occur through a change in the allocation of production costs between owners and tenants. An owner who finds his tax liability increased may decide, for example, to stop providing plowing livestock or to give the tenants less seed than formerly. Although the respective obligations of owners and tenants are usually defined by custom or legislation, it can be presumed that leeway for variations exists in practice. Any leeway will most certainly be under the control of the owner rather than the tenant; thus it will facilitate tax shifting by the former to the latter, but not the reverse.

Another aspect of landlord-tenant relationships warrants attention in this connection. By definition, a true competitive rent is a "rack rent," or a rent which reserves to the owners the maximum possible share of the produce. In the densely populated areas of the world, such a rent would probably be ruthless in its impact on tenants. Rental practices are undeniably harsh in many countries, as evidenced by the miserably low living standards of the tenants and by the necessity for governmental action to protect tenants from excessive exactions. It may nevertheless be true that many landlords in these countries do not exploit their position to the fullest possible extent, but instead collect rents that are less than would be established if the impersonal forces of competition were controlling.[10] The following observation, originally made with reference to landlords in England, may also describe what sometimes happens in underdeveloped countries: "The wish for political power, for personal popularity, for social deference, frequently inclines an owner not to charge all he might for his land. The wish to be considered a good landlord, and the fear to be thought a bad landlord, are powerful motives."[11] Although the high degree of paternalism among English landlords is not typical of the landlord classes in underdeveloped countries, paternalism is still not entirely absent in these countries.

Whenever the actual rent is below a rack rent, owners may take advantage of the opportunity, within the limits of the law, to shift part of a tax increase onto their tenants, provided that the tenants can absorb it without being pushed down to a starvation level. On the other hand, if tenants are the liable taxpayers and their taxes are increased, it would probably be of little avail for them to apply to the owners for more favorable rental terms, unless the tenants have a bargaining weapon in the form of alternative employment possibilities. In the event of rent controls, however, tenants may sometimes gain relief from onerous taxes through the government's lowering of the ceilings.

Occasionally, the law requires the land tax to be divided between the owner and the tenant, as in the Punjab where legislation in 1952 fixed the tenant's share of the total produce at 60 per cent, but at the same time enjoined him to bear a proportionate share of the tax.[12]

In summary, it appears that intrasectoral shifting of land taxes

[10] According to B. Das Gupta, the actual rent tends to be less than a rack rent in India, owing to the influence of customs and law in holding the competition for land in check; see *Provincial Taxation under Autonomy* (Calcutta, 1948), pp. 260–261.

[11] Bagehot, quoted in Seligman, p. 272.

[12] *Progress in Land Reform,* pp. 143–144. According to Lakdawala, pp. 128–129, similar arrangements are in effect in other provinces in India.

assumes practical importance only with respect to the division of the tax between landowning and tenant groups. For a variety of reasons, farm laborers, traders, and moneylenders tend to be insulated from the impact of land taxes. Impersonal economic factors are most likely to be important as determinants of the direction and extent of intrasectoral shifting in countries where land is relatively plentiful and landlords must compete for tenants. A tax on landlords in these countries will tend to remain with them and not be shifted to tenants, except in the unlikely case in which the tax reduced the supply of land under cultivation; whereas a tax on tenants might well be passed on to landlords, because it would tend to discourage some tenants from seeking land to farm. Opposite conclusions are indicated for countries which are land-poor. Their condition may be more conducive to shifting the tax to tenants, unless the latter are protected by governmental regulations.[13] Tax shifting from tenants to owners would not seem likely in these densely populated countries, although governments may compel owners to share in a new tax imposed on tenants.

A Digression on Tax Capitalization

At many points in the preceding analysis it was indicated that the relative immobility of the factors of production in agriculture tends to restrict both intersectoral and intrasectoral shifting of land taxes. To the extent that factor immobility prevents a tax-induced change in the market prices of agricultural products, however, it encourages a tax-induced change in the market price of the income-producing asset, which is land. The latter price change is not a manifestation of tax shifting but of tax capitalization and should be distinguished from shifting.

[13] Although landlords are the liable taxpayers in India, it is generally assumed that tenants share in the tax. Indeed, a common practice is to have the tenants pay the tax on behalf of their landlords. A recent study of the incidence of taxation in India makes the assumption that the land revenue is distributed on a proportional basis among all income groups in the rural sector (*Report of the Taxation Enquiry Commission, 1953–54,* Government of India, 1955, I, 73).

Capitalization is the pricing process for income-yielding assets. In a perfectly competitive market, with buyers and sellers having full knowledge of market conditions, an asset such as land would be valued at a capital sum equivalent to the discounted value of the flow of periodic services which the asset is expected to yield. When the imposition of a tax reduces the value of the expected services to the owner, a person contemplating buying the asset will ordinarily lower his offer price by the amount of the capitalized value of the tax. If he succeeds in buying at this reduced price, he will be able to secure the pre-tax rate of return on his investment. As the new owner, he will pay the tax, but he will be no richer or poorer because of it. When a tax is lowered, capitalization operates in the reverse direction; it permits the seller to obtain a higher price for the asset, thus handing him a windfall, so to speak, and at the same time it deprives the buyer of any benefit from the lower tax.

Capitalization is without much practical significance in many underdeveloped countries, simply because land seldom changes hands, except through gratuitous transfers.

To maintain that a given land tax is capitalized presupposes an active land market, so that land values will reflect market forces rather than noneconomic influences. It also presupposes, first, that the supply of agricultural land is inelastic with respect to changes in the return on land, for otherwise at least part of the tax would be shifted rather than capitalized; second, that the pattern of future tax liabilities is foreseeable and fully anticipated; third, that the government does not spend the tax revenue in a way that affects the value of land services; and fourth, that the tax does not affect the rate at which land income is capitalized. The form of land taxation is not relevant to capitalization, except as the form affects tax shifting.

It would be unusual to find a situation where the necessary conditions for precise tax capitalization are completely satisfied. But whenever the value of land is affected by changes in taxation, at least part of the tax is being capitalized; from this standpoint, therefore, tax capitalization probably is a fairly prevalent phenomenon, no matter how imperfectly it operates. In fact, tax capitalization may be occurring continuously in some countries, simply as a reflection of changing expectations regarding future taxes.

Since capitalization is, in reality, the mechanism of response of land prices to the inability of landowners to shift a tax, it should properly be studied as part of the analysis of tax incidence. No satisfactory solution has been found, however, to the problem of whether (and, if so, how) to allow for tax capitalization in statistical investigations of the distribution of taxes among the population.[14] To the extent that land sales take place only within a single economic group, the impact of tax capitalization will of course be restricted to that group.

[14] See Carl Shoup, "Capitalization and Shifting of the Property Tax," *Property Taxes*, Tax Policy League (New York, 1940), p. 200.

VI

THE VIEWPOINT OF EQUITY (Continued)

THE RELATION between the ultimate burden of taxation and the taxpayers' capacity to carry that burden has deep and broad significance beyond the equity aspects of tax policy decisions. The relation can be studied at the over-all, sectoral, and individual taxpayer levels, according to the analytical purpose which it is intended to serve. At the over-all level, for example, it may be used as evidence of how closely the economically optimum level of taxation is being achieved for the country as a whole.[1] At the sectoral level, the relation of tax incidence, which is the end result of the shifting process, to taxable capacity affords a means of assessing the allocation of taxes among the different productive sectors relative to each sector's potential contribution of resources required for the country's future economic development. Finally, at the individual taxpayer level the relation provides a summary measure of the fairness, or justness, of the distributional pattern of taxation: is the tax incidence apportioned among the population in equitable relationship to individual taxpaying capacity?

This chapter, which concludes the analysis of different methods of land taxation from the viewpoint of equity, focuses on the relation between incidence and taxpaying capacity at the individual taxpayer level. The sectoral and over-all relationships, because they involve problems of aggregative economics, will be studied from the viewpoint of economic policy in Chapter VIII. Keeping these different aspects of tax policy separate is a necessary simplification for analytical purposes, although in reality there is a close interconnection between them. Obviously,

[1] The "optimum level" is defined in the section on "The Level of Taxation," Chapter VIII, below.

the amount of funds which can be transfered with economic advantage from private hands to the government, or from one sector of the private economy to another sector, depends to an important extent on the relative equitableness of the inter-taxpayer distributional pattern of the taxes; similarly, the importance to be attached to the latter pattern varies directly with the aggregate amount of funds being shifted. That is to say, a tax can be expected to have a relatively higher tolerance level, yield-wise, the more equitably it is distributed among the population, while comparatively flagrant inequities might be tolerated, distribution-wise, provided the tax is light.

Relation to Individual Taxpaying Capacity

The fundamental requirements of equity in taxation are suggested by the elementary proposition that an equitable tax is one which satisfies two tests: (1) impartiality among persons in like economic circumstances and (2) reasonable differentiation among persons in unlike circumstances. Before these tests can be put to practical use, an objective and quantitative standard for measuring each individual's "economic circumstances" must be agreed upon.

Measurement of Taxpaying Capacity

The frequency of different tax bases and methods of taxation throughout the world is not a reliable guide to popular thinking as to how to identify persons with similar taxpaying capacity and make a "reasonable" classification of persons with differing capacities. One must look at tax ideals rather than tax practices. Approached in that way, the standard for measuring taxable capacity that attracts wider support than any other, in principle but not necessarily in practice, is the taxpayer's net income. Net wealth (tangible and intangible) is also endorsed by many governments, but more as a means of compensating for observed deficiencies in the measurement of net income than as a criterion in its own right. While certain types of consumption offer unassailable evidence of taxpaying capacity, an individual's total consumption has a significant shortcoming if used for that purpose because it neglects income that is saved.

The measurement of net income for tax purposes raises many economic, legal, and practical issues beyond the scope of this book. Here it will suffice to examine only those aspects of the problem that have particular relevance to the question of devising an equitable method of taxing the agricultural sector in underdeveloped countries.

Definition of Net Income

The rationale behind acceptance of net income as the most nearly ideal basis for the allocation of taxes among individuals is that it provides a comprehensive measure of a person's economic well-being. The definition of net income most appropriate to this usage is the total value of a person's consumption during the given period, increased or reduced by the change in his net wealth.[2] Insofar as an individual earns his livelihood from working the land, his net income would be the difference between the gross value of his harvest and his total production costs (including capital consumption allowances and the cost of borrowed capital, but excluding the value of his own and his family's labor). An agriculturist might also earn income from other sources – for example, from raising livestock or by direct investment of his labor in land improvements. If he owns his dwelling, that is also a source of income. His gross income, adjusted for production costs, necessarily equals his consumption and the increment in his ownership of wealth.

There is no place in the above definition for a distinction between income that results from market transactions and non-

[2] Henry Simons was a leading advocate of this method of defining net income; see his *Personal Income Taxation* (Chicago, 1938), pp. 50–51. For a review of alternate income concepts, see O. H. Brownlee and E. D. Allen, *Economics of Public Finance* (2nd ed.; New York, 1954), pp. 242–247.

money, or imputed, income (that is, income produced and consumed or invested directly by the person himself); both categories are included. In actual income tax legislation, however, the tax base is ordinarily restricted because of administrative considerations to income that is realized by the individual through exchange transactions; this results in exempting from taxation the value of goods and services produced and consumed by the same household. (Similarly, the value of increases in owner-produced wealth is not commonly taxed as income.) When applied to the agricultural sector, the practice of exempting nonmonetary income has a serious drawback, particularly in underdeveloped countries. Where agricultural production is of a predominantly subsistence character, excluding all forms of income in kind appreciably narrows the potential tax base; home-consumed farm produce, for example, probably accounts for two-fifths or more of agricultural income in most of the poorer countries. There are also other important forms of income in kind in the agricultural sector, such as the imputed value of owner-occupied dwellings, fuel gathered by the household, and improvements by owners on their property.[3]

Although certain classes of nonmonetary income may be ignored for tax purposes without seriously violating the net income criterion of taxable capacity, that would not seem to be true of so important a source of agricultural income as the value of food produced and consumed by the taxpayer and his family.

The relation of nonmonetary income to taxable capacity has another facet, however, which has considerable practical importance for the problem of allocating taxes among farmers. In most countries having net income taxes, provision is made for

[3] In the *Report of the Taxation Enquiry Commission, 1953–54* (Government of India, 1955), 45 per cent of the total value of consumption in the rural sector of India is represented by imputed value. The proportion of home-produced food in total food consumption is 63 per cent; for fuel and light the corresponding proportion is 70 per cent. Home-produced food alone accounts for an estimated 40 per cent of total consumption in the rural sector (vol. I, pp. 63–66). The Commission's estimates are based on the fourth round schedules of the National Sample Survey.

personal exemptions which vary according to the taxpayer's marital status and the number of his dependents. The purpose of such exemptions is partly administrative, since it would not be feasible to assess and collect an income tax on every income recipient, no matter how small his income, and partly for the promotion of equity. In the latter case the exemptions are an expression of the appealing view that persons at the bottom of the income scale should be relieved of taxation whenever feasible and that others should be allowed a tax reduction according to their respective family obligations.

The reasoning behind personal exemptions suggests a provocative line of argument leading to the conclusion that the exclusion of nonmonetary income from the tax base may sometimes serve much the same purpose in promoting taxpayer equity in the agricultural sector as personal exemptions do in the industrial sector. This argument begins with the observation that farmers growing food crops ordinarily will grow enough to feed themselves and their families before selling produce in the market, while farmers growing other crops are usually able to set aside some land for a family garden. In both cases, it might be claimed, the presence of cash income probably indicates production in excess of basic food requirements; conversely, where there is no cash income, there is small likelihood of any excess over these requirements. On the strength of such reasoning, and taking into account the acknowledged desirability of protecting the living standards of the lowest income groups to the fullest possible extent, one might be persuaded that taxable capacity in the agricultural sector can be gauged with reasonable accuracy by the amount of cash income alone, and that no grave injustice is inflicted when non-cash income is ignored for tax purposes.

How defensible is this argument? In the first place, a decision on a subsistence exemption is dependent upon fiscal and economic, as well as humanitarian, considerations. Strictly speaking, the cost of government is an element in subsistence, and to relieve some families of the burden of sharing in that cost is the equivalent of a subsidy which some governments are able to afford more easily than others. Second, the nonmonetary sector in agriculture is not necessarily an exclusively subsistence economy. Sumptuous living may be supported on a nonmonetary basis, with servants paid in kind, food plentiful and consumed lavishly, liquor home-brewed, and textiles woven and sewn at home. Persons in these circumstances may have taxable capacity far beyond their cash income. Moreover, food may sometimes be available in excess of immediate consumption requirements and yet never reach markets because of inadequate marketing facilities. In the third place, the assumption that nonmonetary income is distributed evenly throughout the agricultural sector may be quite unwarranted. The exclusion of unequally distributed nonmonetary income from the tax base would affect the distributional pattern very differently than would a system of personal exemptions. As a general rule, a farmer growing his own food will eat better, the richer his land. Moreover, agricultural production usually is market-oriented to a greater extent in some sections of a country than in other sections, thus causing large variations in cash income which do not correspond to differences in real income. For example, farmers near a large city often find it profitable to specialize in growing vegetables and other cash crops and to purchase grain in the market place. Having relatively little nonmonetary income, such farmers require considerable cash income merely to cover their subsistence needs.

Perhaps for the mass of farmers in a large number of countries, no serious injustice would be involved if nonmonetary income were ignored and only cash income taxed. It is conceivable, too, that the tax system in agriculture can be accommodated to a cash income standard by introducing special tax provisions for those farmers who do not fit into the general pattern; for example, vegetable and fruit growers might be taxed on a different basis than that used for taxing producers of basic crops such as rice. Nevertheless, there is no gainsaying the conceptual superiority of an income concept that is more inclusive than cash income.

The narrower concept, because it involves a compromising of the basic standard for measuring taxpaying capacity, is defensible only if it offers compensating advantages in meeting other objectives.

In connection with the above consideration of the tax treatment of nonmonetary income, it should be noted that the ordinary type of land tax that is assessed according to the productive capacity or market value of the land does not differentiate between produce that is sold and produce that is consumed at home. The tax base for that type of tax, however, is usually a variant of gross income or rental value, rather than of net income. Marketing taxes, on the other hand, are levies on gross cash income and ignore nonmonetary income.

Application of Net Income Criterion

A decision to accept net income as the most appropriate single yardstick of an individual's capacity to pay taxes has several corollaries in the form of guiding principles with respect to the practical application of the net income standard. Needless to say, equity requirements are more likely to be satisfied if the taxes are distributed according to the ascertained rather than the presumptive net income of the taxpayer; when presumptive assessment is an administrative necessity, as is often the case, its equitableness will depend on how closely the assessment approximates, or is correlated with, actual net income. Many practices associated with presumptive assessments, such as the determination of production costs on the basis of averages for all producers instead of on the basis of each producer's experience, probably result in a tax base that varies more closely with gross income than with net income. Yet from an equity standpoint, gross income may prove a poor substitute for net income, since the ratio of production costs to gross income will fluctuate with such factors as the quality and topography of the land, the availability of irrigation, and distance from distribution centers.

Families living at a bare subsistence level – which may be

defined more liberally in some countries than in others — should not be taxed. A minimum exemption — on a flat basis, or better still, in accordance with family size — can be recommended simply on humanitarian grounds if for no other reasons. As already noted, the exclusion of home-consumed produce from the tax base may take the place of a minimum exemption in some countries. Personal exemptions may not be feasible, or appropriate, under a marketing tax, however, except that home-consumed produce will not be subject to the tax.

Strict adherence to an accounting period as short as a calendar or crop year is not likely to prove equitable as between stable and fluctuating incomes, especially when losses are interspersed with profits. The preferred method of meeting this problem is through loss carry-overs or a system of averaging, although some countries attempt to reduce the inequities by means of *ad hoc* tax relief.

The arguments in favor of net income as a better index of taxpaying capacity than other tax bases do not offer much guidance as to the nature of the relationship between net income and taxpaying capacity. A proportionate relationship would justify a proportionate tax, but if capacity is viewed as increasing more rapidly than income, the optimum tax rate schedule would be progressive.[4] No one is likely to quarrel with the proposition that a taxpayer with, say, twice the income of another has at least twice the ability to pay taxes; to go further and claim that he has more than twice the ability brings up the question "how much more?" Progressive tax rates seem to be intuitively attractive to many people, but to attempt to specify the desirable degree of progression raises the equalitarian issue which, in the final analysis, is a problem in social ethics that each country has to solve for itself.

There are many instances of sharp modification of the equity standard in the interest of supervening economic objectives. "Tax-

[4] If there is a minimum income exemption, the effective rate will be progressive even though the stated rate is proportional.

payers who are otherwise in identical circumstances with respect to income or wealth and family status may nonetheless be treated differently either (a) by penalty taxes, if they hold land idle or reap speculative gains from it, or (b) by special concessions, if they pursue favored land uses (e.g., grow desired crops) or make improvements and investments in their land. Impartiality, of course, can still govern within the structure of any one of these intrusions [on the equity principle]."[5] The logic of modifications of this type is in the belief that an immediate sacrifice of equity will promote a higher goal from which all will benefit.

Equity Aspects of Specific Types of Taxes

To measure accurately the degree of compliance of each specific type of land tax with equity criteria would require extremely difficult empirical testings. A set of statistical comparisons of the average tax burden under each type of tax for persons at different levels of income would be needed. The burden would need to be measured after taking into account such tax shifting as is believed likely to occur. At most the present study can only suggest how the form of the tax and the manner in which it is administered can affect its equitableness.

The survey in Chapter I classifies the main systems of land taxation according to whether the tax base is land area, a rental value concept, or an income concept. Looking simply at their external form, one would ordinarily expect to find that the land taxes which employ an income concept are the ones most likely to achieve the closest approximation to the standard of equity set forth above. Among the taxes in this category are a few which are actually allocated according to net income. In the present section attention will first be given to these few taxes, in order to determine whether they express the proposed equity standard as closely in fact as they do in form; next, the section will assess the equity aspects of land taxes which have other bases.

[5] Walter W. Heller "A Survey of Agricultural Taxation and Economic Development," *Papers and Proceedings of the Conference on Agricultural Taxation and Economic Development* (Cambridge, 1954), pp. 149–150.

Net Income Base. When agriculture is taxed according to net income, the tax in question is usually part of a general income tax of either the global or schedular type and therefore does not have the distinguishing characteristics of land taxation, such as *in rem* form or cadastral assessment. Only a few rather obscure land taxes with a net income base were identified in Chapter I. One of these is found in Nigeria, where the tax is initially assessed communally according to the estimated yield of the land controlled by each village, and then apportioned among the inhabitants of each village on the basis of rudimentary local estimates of net income. This method of land taxation would seem to be appropriate only in countries where the population is organized on a communal basis and considerable authority is concentrated in the village heads. The method requires each village community to accept joint responsibility for collecting the tax from its members; the members, in turn, must be prepared to accept the allocation of taxes that is decided upon by the governing council. If administered in a true spirit of fairness by benevolent officials, a tax of this type could provide a model of equitable assessment; in the hands of malevolent officials, however, the tax would be a powerful instrument of oppression.

Another example of assessment according to a net income concept is the land tax in Madras, India, where the average productive capacity of each field is determined and expressed in monetary terms, and the "net produce" is obtained by deducting estimated expenses of cultivation from the gross produce. In accordance with the net income concept, no deduction is allowed for value of the labor of the cultivator and his family. The land tax in Madras is not based on ascertained net income, however, since the tax is assessed without reference to the individual taxpayer's actual receipts and disbursements for the taxable period. In fact, the tax assessment is not even adjusted for fluctuations in production between good and bad years; once the tax is "settled," it remains in effect for about thirty years. "Net produce" is determined according to a schedule of hypothetical yields of certain staple crops on each grade of land, without regard to the crops actually grown or to each farmer's productive ability and industriousness. The commutation price for converting physical units into monetary values is not an actual price; instead, the average price of the preceding twenty non-famine years is used. The allowances for production costs are standardized and do not necessarily accord with the actual expenses of individual farmers. No allowance is made for interest costs, nor is any differentiation made according to whether the owner leases the land or works it himself.[6]

Apart from the possibility that the settlement officers may fail to carry out their assigned task satisfactorily, there are two general reasons why a tax of the type used in Madras falls short of meeting equity criteria. The first is the failure to adjust the assessments more frequently. If prices should tumble, for example, the tax assessment might absorb an exceedingly large share of the current year's income. In view of the many changes in production and prices that are certain to occur with the passage of time, the assessments are likely to become less equitable the longer they remain unchanged. Moreover, at any given time one might expect to find flagrant inequities between assessments that are twenty or thirty years old and assessments that are recent. The second broad reason why individual taxpayers may receive unfair treatment is that the tax is completely impersonal. Implicit in its design is the assumption that taxable capacity is derived from the qualities of the soil and is independent of each taxpayer's economic circumstances and of the income he actually earns from working the land.

On the other hand, the tax in Madras embodies assessment features which are sensitive to equity criteria: the method of settlement aims to allow for differences in the productive capacity of each field and adjustments are made for cost disparities on different grades of soil. Evidently, the tax could produce

[6] A short description of the tax in Madras is given in the *Report of the Taxation Enquiry Commission, 1953–54,* III, 186, 268–269.

equitable results in a static economy in which the land was owner-cultivated and the farmers were all of equal skill and followed standardized methods of cultivation. In short, the Madras tax contains some of the foundations of a highly equitable tax arrangement, because it focuses upon the net income potential of the land.

Gross Income Base. The tithe affords another example of why the definition of the tax base is not always a reliable guide to the relative degree of compliance of a tax with equity criteria. Certain features mentioned above as sources of inequitable treatment under the land tax in Madras are not present in the tithe, which is levied on the actual harvest as assessed in the field and has the advantages of being contingent upon an ascertained value and of being responsive to changes in production and prices. Especially in a developing economy, the distributional pattern of a well-administered tithe may correspond more closely with the distribution of taxable capacity than would the pattern resulting under a tax of the type found in Madras, despite the fact that the tithe ignores differences in costs of production while the tax in Madras presumably contains refined allowances for such differences.

An alternative application of the gross income base is found in mainland China and in the Republic of Korea, where the assessment is based upon the estimated "normal" yield. However, the failure to adjust the assessment each year as the results of the harvest become available deprives this type of tax of the advantage of flexibility which is present under a tithe. In some areas where the gross income base is found, a basic exemption is recognized and the tax rates are graduated. Such provisions help to moderate the objectionable features of the gross income base.

Broadly speaking, the difference between the relative equitableness of gross and net bases of assessment will not be large in countries where the land under cultivation is of even quality and where location is not an important determinant of land value, for in that case unit costs of production will be substantially the same on one field as on the next; but if lands of widely dissimilar grades are being farmed, it is possible that major differences will arise between the distributional patterns under each tax base. One would also expect to find that the gross income base can be applied with greater equitableness in economies dominated by a single crop than where agriculture is diversified.

Marketed Produce as Tax Base. In certain respects, a tax on marketed produce has unique qualifications as an instrument of equitable taxation. It is the close equivalent of a tax on cash income and has in its favor, therefore, the arguments already deduced in support of a cash income concept. Moreover, the tax is responsive to changes in production and prices. The Taxation Enquiry Commission of the Government of India summarized the justification for this type of tax thus: ". . . the incidence of such a tax, as distinguished from that of land revenue, will be appropriately heavy on the larger landholders, while the small landholder, to the extent his crop is consumed and not sold by him, will not have to bear the tax at all."[7] The Commission found the tax seriously objectionable, however, on administrative grounds.

A disadvantage of a marketing tax is that it falls on high-cost and low-cost producers alike. The tax would also seem to be unduly harsh on farmers who do not produce basic food crops and must, therefore, market their produce in order to obtain cash for purchasing food. Forward shifting of the marketing tax to consumers would not eliminate the latter source of inequitableness.

Annual Value and Capital Value Bases. The underlying objective of the large and important group of land taxes employing a rental value concept, expressed either as annual or capital value, is to assess the taxable capacity of the land itself, as distinguished from the capacity of the owners of the land. As shown in Chapter I, such a distinction is counterfeit; the concept of taxable capacity is meaningful only if interpreted in relation to persons, not things. On the other hand, the taxable capacity of a landlord whose entire

[7] Vol. III, p. 209.

income is derived from rentals on land which is owned outright would seem to be identical with the net rental value of his land. As applied to such individuals, therefore, the use of a rental value basis of taxation might be reasonably consistent with equity considerations, provided the tax is assessed properly and it is not shifted. Still, there is nothing in this argument to justify holding the tax constant from one year to the next or levying both a land tax and an income tax on the same income. If landlords succeed in shifting the tax to tenants, however, the initial relationship to taxpaying capacity will be destroyed. The rental value concept does not seem to be appropriate as a measure of the taxable capacity of either a tenant or an owner-cultivator. Rental payments are likely to be related more closely to a tenant's gross income than to his net income, while in the case of an owner-cultivator, net income includes, in addition to land rent, the return on his own labor, capital, and entrepreneurship.

With these taxes, as with the types previously considered, so many factors other than the definition of the tax base enter into an evaluation of their relative equitableness that it can be misleading to place heavy stress on the appropriateness of the statutory base as an index of a person's taxable capacity. The accuracy of the assessments, the frequency of reassessments, the effectiveness of tax collection, and arrangements for tax relief in years of poor harvest, rather than the tax base identified in the law, may prove to be the crucial determinants of the distributional pattern under each tax.

Although both the annual value and capital value bases of assessment incorporate a rental value concept, there are several differences in the relative equitableness of the two methods.[8] Among the arguments advanced in favor of the use of annual rental value rather than capital value are the following: [9] (1) an annual value tax does not tax expected earnings which are never

[8] See Chapter I, pp. 23–27.

[9] The respective advantages of each approach are analyzed in M. Slade Kendrick, *Taxation Issues* (New York, 1933), pp. 66ff.

realized (but such expectations are ordinarily capitalized in the market); (2) it avoids the hardship which taxpayers may experience in meeting taxes which are out of proportion to current income; (3) it eliminates over-taxation of deferred-income properties, such as land producing bush or tree crops (olives, dates, copra, rubber, coffee, cacao, tea, figs, etc.)[10]; and (4) it avoids the injustices which arise under the capital value method when, as a matter of custom or for other noneconomic reasons, different classes of land are capitalized at different rates. On the other hand, there is at least one argument in favor of the capital value base as the more equitable of the two: idle land, which may have considerable market value, is not usually taxed under the annual value method but is taxed when capital value is used as the base. Ownership of idle land may sometimes be indicative of taxable capacity, even though the land is not currently producing income.

Area Base. The neglect of equity considerations is most conspicuous in the case of land taxes based on area. It is necessary to distinguish, however, between those area taxes which recognize only a gross classification of land — as between fertile and barren land, for example — and other types which provide many separate rate classifications. Efficient administration of the tax in West Jordan, for example, where there are sixteen rate classifications according to land fertility and use, might produce more equitable results than would a less well-administered tax with a statutory base more in harmony with equity criteria.

Summary and Conclusions

The viewpoint of equity is one of several guideposts along the path to a rational policy of land taxation. It is a difficult guidepost to read, however, because equity expresses intangible values

[10] It can be demonstrated that the total amount of tax paid over a given number of years under a capital value basis will be heavier on properties with delayed income than on properties of equivalent value yielding income in every year. This type of inequity is not present under an annual value basis. See Fred R. Fairchild, *Forest Taxation in the United States,* U. S.

and because its application requires firm knowledge of the distributional patterns of different taxes in relation to the distribution of taxpaying capacity among the population.

"Searching for the taxpayer," which was the subject of Chapter V, involves the application of basic theoretical principles of tax shifting to particular types of taxes as administered in a given economic and institutional setting. An assessment of the probability of tax shifting should allow for the many barriers to the free operation of market forces in underdeveloped countries. Where these barriers are grounded in local customs and in an insensitivity of the population to economic inducements, they may prevent both intersectoral and intrasectoral shifting. Where an inordinate amount of economic power is concentrated in the hands of particular individuals or groups, however, the extent and direction of tax shifting – especially between landlords and tenants – may be subject to private control. On the other hand, the barriers may take the form of government controls, in which event it might be possible to regulate tax shifting in order to achieve a desired distributional pattern.

The present chapter has explored the equity aspects of specific types of land taxes. The basic standard against which these aspects were judged is the commonplace rule that taxes should be distributed as nearly as possible in relation to each taxpayer's economic well-being. Net income was selected as the most appropriate distributional standard, but other criteria of equitableness often deserve recognition, too. The determinants of the relative equitableness of different taxes were shown to be allied more closely to the practices adopted in the interest of administrative and fiscal expediency, than to the formal structure of the taxes. Furthermore, the actual conditions of agricultural production in each country have an important bearing upon the equitableness of any given method of land taxation.

Although the preceding analysis supports few dogmatic con-

Department of Agriculture, Miscellaneous Publication No. 218 (October 1935), pp. 39–47.

clusions as to the superiority of certain taxes over others, the analysis aids in identifying those tax features which promote greater equitableness and those which have the opposite effect. For example, a tax that is personal, in that it differentiates among individuals according to several indicia of taxpaying capacity, and is responsive to changes in production and prices would seem to be preferable from the viewpoint of equity to one that is impersonal and invariable over long periods of time.

Out of necessity, the approach in this chapter has been to test the equitableness of different land taxes, apart from the distributional pattern of the tax system as a whole. It should be emphasized, however, that equitableness must ultimately be tested against the latter pattern. Alfred Marshall argued that point cogently, as follows: "Onerous taxes, imperial and local, must be treated as a whole. Almost every onerous tax taken by itself presses with undue weight on some class or other; but this is of no moment if the inequalities of each are compensated by those of others, and variations in the several parts synchronise. If that difficult condition is satisfied, the system may be equitable, though any one part of it regarded alone would be inequitable." [11]

[11] Quoted in A. C. Pigou, *A Study in Public Finance* (3rd ed.; London, 1949), pp. 56–57.

VII

OBJECTIVES OF AGRICULTURAL DEVELOPMENT

THE VALUE of economic policy as a guide to the selection of the most suitable methods of taxation is greatly enhanced when the policy objectives are fitted into a comprehensive development plan and spelled out in detail rather than expressed simply in loose and general terms. In many countries, however, the only clearly explicit economic goal is increased total production. So broad a policy objective is not especially helpful to those responsible for integrating tax policy with over-all economic policy, since it fails to indicate what specific types of production should be increased and what kinds of resource transfers will be needed. It is a mistake to assume that increased production, regardless of its composition and source, is necessarily synonymous with increased national welfare; furthermore, it should be recognized that certain patterns of increases can contribute more than other patterns can to a country's long-run growth and stability. Selected production cutbacks, as well as increases, often have a place in a development plan.

A few countries – India is an outstanding present-day example – have developed their economic planning to the point where it has direct relevance to decisions on tax policy.[1] Goals have been established for each major component of the national product, such as investment, consumption, imports, and exports, for several years ahead. These goals have been translated into specific production objectives for government and private industry, re-

[1] See *Report of the Taxation Enquiry Commission, 1953–54* (Government of India, 1955), I, 85–143.

spectively, in each important economic sector: for example, in agriculture, mining, manufacturing, public utilities, transportation, trade, and government. Guided by that type of economic blueprint, a government can proceed to design measures to aid in mobilizing the required resources and directing them into the desired channels. An appropriate plan of taxation can help to assure the success of such an effort. Not only is taxation a major method of diverting domestic savings into development projects, but it is also a means of influencing the volume and intensity of use of resources in the different sectors of the private economy.

The purpose of this chapter is to clarify the viewpoint of economic policy, insofar as it is applicable to decisions regarding land taxation, by identifying and briefly examining the main goals for the agricultural sector in underdeveloped countries.[2] The specific ways in which the method of land taxation might be related to the realization of these goals are analyzed in the next chapter.

Because economic circumstances differ so radically from country to country, there are but few policy objectives which are appropriate for the agricultural sectors of all underdeveloped countries under all conceivable conditions. The objective of increasing total agricultural production may be close to being a universal aim (outside of some developed countries), yet it would not be surprising to find a country which places a heavy emphasis on industrialization and therefore chooses to forgo possible increases in agricultural output in order to obtain more rapid growth elsewhere.

Perhaps the only important agricultural goal which is suitable under all conditions is that of improved efficiency in the use of

[2] This chapter draws extensively upon the papers by Gustav V. Papanek, "Development Problems Relevant to Agricultural Tax Policy," and Walter W. Heller, "The Use of Agricultural Taxation for Incentive Purposes," in *Papers and Proceedings of the Conference on Agricultural Taxation and Economic Development* (Cambridge, 1954), pp. 189–244. See also *Essential Steps in National Agricultural Improvement*, Development Paper No. 3, Food and Agriculture Organization of the United Nations (April 1950).

agricultural resources. Any policy that would raise efficiency, and thus enable a country to obtain a larger amount of production from a given input of resources, would appear to be necessarily consistent with that country's development plan, regardless of whether the plan provides for an expanding, contracting, or essentially stable agricultural sector. Most of the other goals surveyed below, while vital to many countries, cannot be recommended for any individual country without first being tested against the requirements of that country's over-all development plan.

Increasing the Efficiency of Production

Governmental policy may focus upon various possible methods of increasing the efficiency of agricultural production. Increased water use often is considered to be one of the most promising methods, both because of its direct effect on crop yields and because it is likely to be a prerequisite for the application of other techniques of agricultural improvement, such as increased use of fertilizer. Adoption of improved production techniques, such as crop rotation and more efficient cultivation, the introduction of improved seed and better strains of breeding stock, and the encouragement of more widespread use of farm implements are additional measures which might aid in raising efficiency. More adequate agricultural credit facilities and more satisfactory organizational arrangements for the distribution of production requisites and the marketing of crops also might help. Finally, efficiency might be advanced through numerous possible changes in the land tenure system — for example, through consolidation of uneconomic production units or curtailment of absentee ownership.

The goal of increased productive efficiency need not be interpreted exclusively in terms of the input-output ratios for individual crops; it can also refer to the over-all pattern of resource use within agriculture. Changes in the composition of production – such as a shift from, say, rice to other grains, or a diversion of productive activity to new crops or livestock products in which the country seems to have a comparative advantage over other producers – may rank high on the list of a country's agricultural objectives. Such changes may increase the total value of agricultural production, without necessarily involving a larger drain on the country's resources, and may yield other benefits, such as expanded foreign trade and increased stability of the economy as a whole.

For a country to attain a high degree of efficiency in agriculture, farmers must be instilled with the necessary economic ambitions. In some underdeveloped countries, however, there is evidence that many farmers do not have a strong and active interest in producing much more than the basic subsistence requirements of their families and themselves.[3] The strengthening of economic motives often is a central objective of governmental policy in these countries; unless farmers produce substantially more than their own needs, an industrial sector cannot be supported.

These different methods of raising productive efficiency in agriculture merit close attention when land tax policy is being formulated. Almost all the methods will entail either larger investment or a redirection of existing investment, and tax policy can serve such ends by making more funds available for financing development programs and by increasing the relative attractiveness of some forms of private investment over other forms and over other possible uses of income. In addition, a desired redirection of agricultural production can sometimes be effectively stimulated by favorable combinations of penalties and rewards provided by tax legislation.

It is conceivable that in some countries the major potential contribution of tax policy to increased efficiency is through the removal of obstacles imposed by the existing level and form of

[3] Many different explanations have been offered as to why the drive for material gains is noticeably weaker in some underdeveloped countries than in most Western capitalist societies. See Heller, pp. 234–237.

taxation, rather than through the introduction of positive tax incentives. Many specific examples of the relationship of land tax policy to productive efficiency are given in the next chapter.

Bringing Additional Resources into Production

Agricultural production can be increased not merely through improved efficiency, but also by attracting additional resources into productive uses. Most underdeveloped countries would probably like to accomplish as much as possible in both these directions, provided that the desired results could be achieved without depriving nonagricultural sectors of the economy of needed resources. There would be small likelihood of adverse effects on other sectors if previously idle or undercultivated land were drawn into agricultural production. Before taking steps to channel additional labor, raw materials, or capital funds into agricultural uses, however, a government should determine whether the resources would otherwise find employment outside agriculture and, if so, whether the country stands to gain or lose by having them put to use in agriculture.

In countries such as India and Pakistan, where there are tremendous reservoirs of idle manpower in the agricultural sector, increased production as a result of fuller utilization of labor resources would certainly represent a net gain to the economy. At the other extreme are those countries – Nicaragua and, possibly, Chile are examples – where manpower and other resources are being relatively fully employed, making it necessary to balance potential production gains and losses carefully against each other before any decisions regarding desirable resource transfers are made.

For obvious reasons the optimum development of productive resources can be determined most satisfactorily in the context of a formal economic development plan setting forth annual output goals for all economic sectors in relation to available resources. The plan should indicate what types of agricultural production should be increased and what resources should be drawn upon in order to serve the country's best interests. Tax policy could then be formulated so that it expressed these specific objectives to the fullest possible extent.

Transferring Resources to Nonagricultural Sectors

A closely related phase of government's economic policy toward agriculture concerns transfers of resources from agriculture to other sectors. Transfers from private to government uses are the essence of the taxing and spending process, but many such transfers are not intersectoral. If taxes paid by agriculture are spent on irrigation projects, for example, there is no transfer of resources out of the sector; the effect would be to increase total output — provided, of course, that the projects were economically sound — and probably to alter the composition of output in the direction of reducing the relative share of consumption and increasing that of investment. On the other hand, the government may collect taxes from agricultural producers and invest the proceeds in the industrial sector, thereby inducing a resource shift out of agriculture.[4]

A policy of promoting rural-to-urban transfers often is well suited to the needs of countries seeking means of accelerating their economic development. Not only is it common to find large pools of surplus manpower in the agricultural sectors of underdeveloped countries, but also, at least in the early stages of development, opportunitics for raising productivity and releasing resources for employment elsewhere tend to be larger in agriculture than in other parts of the economy.[5]

[4] W. Arthur Lewis cites the Gold Coast, Burma, and Uganda as modern examples of countries whose governments have used revenues collected in the agricultural sector to finance economic development in other sectors (*The Theory of Economic Growth,* Homewood, Illinois, 1955, p. 231). Japan is the classical historical example; see Herbert Norman, *Japan's Emergence as a Modern State* (Institute of Pacific Relations, New York, 1946).

[5] The theoretical case for intersectoral transfers is forcefully presented in

The success of a program of moving surplus labor off the farms often requires that it be coupled with policies for withdrawing the food formerly consumed by such labor when it was part of the farm community. If the food is not drawn off as the workers move out, living standards would rise in farm areas and decline in cities, and a point might be reached at which a reverse flow of labor back to the farms would be stimulated. Actually, the need for larger flows of agricultural output to nonfarm markets is a long-standing problem for many underdeveloped countries, although it becomes more urgent, of course, when there is a population shift to the cities. Apart from taking direct steps to induce farmers to sell a larger share of their output, a government may wish to encourage more diversified production, in the hope of thereby promoting the growth of commercial crops.[6]

Tax policy can be of considerable assistance to governments attempting to spur economic development by means of intersectoral transfers of the types just described. As a general goal, such governments should aim to collect additional taxes from sectors from which the resources are to be withdrawn and to refrain from overburdening those in which the resources are to be absorbed. In addition, full advantage should be taken of opportunities for designing taxes which provide positive inducements to the desired shifts.[7]

It would be a serious mistake, however, to assume that transfers of resources in the magnitude likely to be needed for more rapid economic development can be achieved through tax policy alone. Many additional governmental measures will ordinarily be required, such as government construction of housing and other community facilities in areas where expansion is sought, and government provision of financial assistance to new industries. Realistically viewed, the most that can be expected from tax

---

Ragnar Nurkse, *Problems of Capital Formation in Underdeveloped Countries* (Oxford, 1953), ch. ii.

[6] See Heller, p. 230.

[7] Nonfiscal applications of land taxes are examined in Chapter XI.

policy in this connection is to have it serve efficiently in a supporting role, rather than as the primary policy instrument, in effecting the necessary resource transfers. Furthermore, tax incentives for resource transfers are likely to be more effective in a growing economy, when the transfers might help to reinforce the growth process, than in a static one.

Welfare Objectives

Finally, there are various objectives relating to the economic welfare of the agricultural sector as a whole or of particular groups within that sector. These objectives have become increasingly prominent on government agenda in recent years, especially in countries governed by democratically elected officials, and have an important bearing upon several aspects of land taxation.

Although welfare objectives are rooted in humanitarian considerations, they are integrally related to national economic policy. The oft-espoused objective of reduced income disparities among the agricultural population provides an apt illustration of this close relationship. Many governments are convinced of the desirability and urgency of income redistribution as a purely humanitarian measure. Whatever steps they take toward that end, however, must of necessity be tempered by a careful regard for the effects of income redistribution on the functioning of the agricultural sector and on capital accumulation. If the effects proved seriously adverse, even the most equalitarian-minded government could not afford to ignore them for long. On the other hand, if favorable economic effects were indicated, a government might endorse the goal of reduced disparities even though it were ordinarily inclined to be callous with respect to the economic plight of its less fortunate citizens.

To improve land tenure arrangements is another example of a policy aim which often gains support from either economic or welfare considerations or from a combination of the two. The ultimate goal may have many different facets: to give tenants a larger share of the total output, to make their tenure more secure, to enhance their personal status in the community, or to increase productive efficiency and expand total output.

All countries are certainly aware of the desirability of raising the general living standards of the agricultural population, but some countries pursue this objective more vigorously than others. As a rule, living standards tend to be substantially lower in agriculture than in other sectors of the economy, and "purely economic" as well as humanitarian considerations argue for concerted governmental action to improve agriculture's position.[8] Just how much of an increase in agricultural income is feasible depends upon such factors as a country's endowment of human and natural resources and the interrelationship between improved conditions in agriculture and the national welfare as a whole.

When agriculturalists live in deep poverty, their health may be undermined to such an extent that their work efficiency suffers. Furthermore, the low income may prevent the replacement of productive capital. These are extreme examples of what might happen on a strictly economic plane when the level of taxation, by pressing unduly against capacity to pay taxes, takes too deep a bite out of agricultural income. That poverty also takes a heavy toll in human suffering is self-evident.

It should be apparent that any substantial realization of these welfare objectives will often be impossible in the absence of accomplishment toward the production goals described earlier; on the other hand, failure to push ahead with welfare programs may seriously impede progress toward the other goals.

In addition to doing all in their power to set the development process in motion, many countries today face a difficult problem in deciding what policy to follow with respect to anticipated increases in production: how much of the increase should be per-

[8] For a comprehensive study of the income ratios between agriculture and industry throughout the world see J. R. Bellerby, *Agriculture and Industry Relative Income* (London, 1956).

mitted to go to consumption, and thereby contribute at once to higher standards of living, and how much to investment, with a promise of improved levels of living at a future date? The manner in which economic and welfare considerations are harmonized in the answers to these questions has a direct bearing upon many decisions in the tax field, especially upon those relating to the distribution of the tax burden and the desirable degree of responsiveness of the tax yield to changes in income.

VIII

THE VIEWPOINT OF ECONOMIC POLICY

TAXATION MAY influence the functioning of the economy in many different ways, some easily recognizable and others subtle and complex. The imposition of a tax may, for example, alter the relative attractiveness to taxpayers of different kinds of economic pursuits; or it may induce changes in the spending and saving patterns of producers and consumers, thereby affecting the level and composition of the national product. Depending upon the form and magnitude of the tax, its economic effects may be confined to limited segments of the economy, or they may fan out across the economy, spreading from one segment to another in the fashion of a chain reaction. Because the economic effects of taxation occur whether or not they are intended, obviously the prudent course for a government is always to give due consideration to the viewpoint of economic policy in its decisions on tax policy.

It should go without saying that whenever possible a government should avoid tax measures with undesirable economic effects and give preference to those with desirable ones. This seemingly self-evident principle — which simply argues for a tax policy that is integrated with economic planning — is often disregarded, perhaps because of unawareness of or uncertainty over the economic effects of taxation, or perhaps in the spurious belief that taxes are for revenue purposes and nothing more.

The apparently hesitant acceptance of the viewpoint of economic policy as a necessary guide to tax policy is all the more difficult to comprehend because most governments at one time or another have made deliberate use of particular taxes with the intent of accomplishing limited economic objectives apart from the goal of raising revenue. This selective application of taxation as an instrument of economic policy is commonly referred to as "incentive" or "regulatory" taxation.[1]

It should be apparent that the viewpoint of economic policy – as expressed in terms of specific economic objectives for the agricultural sector – is highly relevant to many of the key decisions regarding the level, form, and structure of land taxation. In the first section below, attention will be given to the problem of determining the appropriate level of land taxation. Subsequent sections will be devoted to the economic implications of the definition of the tax base, the distributional pattern, structural flexibility, and tax collections in kind.

Optimum Level of Land Taxation

Economic policy considerations provide some obvious overall guides to the optimum level of taxation. They warn against too light and too heavy taxation. Taxation is too light when, by failing to release adequate resources for governmental programs, it contributes to inflation. Taxation is too heavy when it curtails some taxpayers' incomes below subsistence requirements, thereby impairing their health and work efficiency, or when it prevents full utilization of productive resources or the replacement and accumulation of needed productive capital. Merely to define these lower and upper boundaries, however, is not much of an advance, because the range of possible tax levels within the boundaries ordinarily is very wide. How might the range be narrowed with the help of additional economic criteria?

Taxable capacity can be defined as that amount of purchasing power which might be diverted with economic advantage from

[1] Some prominent examples are Australia's graduated tax on unimproved land values, Chile's penalty tax on newly planted vineyards, Argentina's tax on absentee landlords, and the progressive land value increment taxes in Denmark and Portugal. The opportunities for such nonfiscal applications of land taxes are discussed in Chapter XI.

private hands to the government. Capacity may not exist for financing government expenditures of low priority — because of the possibility that the funds would serve higher priority needs if left in private hands than if diverted to the government — and yet may be ample for financing highly essential government programs.

The concept of an economically optimum level of taxation can be derived from the above definition of taxable capacity. As a goal, taxation should be expanded to the point where the available taxable capacity is all being absorbed; by definition, the level of taxation would then be most consistent with the optimum allocation of productive resources throughout the economy. As applied to the land tax, the optimum level is the one which, in conjunction with all other other taxes and a given plan of government spending, would achieve the desired transfer of resources from private to public programs.

It is probably more realistic to think of several relatively separate pools of taxpaying capacity existing within a country, rather than only a single pool from which all taxes draw. Within the agricultural sector, for example, entrepreneurial earnings may comprise one source of taxpaying capacity, rental incomes (cash or imputed) a second source, wage income a third, and accumulated savings a fourth. Moreover, some of these individual sources may themselves be compartmentalized; for example, it may be advisable in some countries to identify two essentially separate sources of entrepreneurial earnings according to whether the earnings accrue to large or small producers. Although the individual pools of taxpaying capacity will often be interconected, so that a tax which draws directly upon one pool will indirectly create a drain upon others, it is extremely unlikely that the economic adjustments set into motion when a tax is imposed will operate so as to equalize the drain of taxation upon them all. Institutional arrangements and economic rigidities of various sorts will obstruct the tax-induced flow of funds from one pool to another and may even block it.

When a country's development plan calls for an expanding agricultural sector, the land tax should be set so as not to release any resources required to support the desired expansion. More specifically, the tax should not prevent increased private investment in agriculture (except in the event that the development plan calls for the substitution of government investment for private investment, or in the event that the investment is of the wrong type); nor should the tax be so burdensome that work efficiency is impaired or land is withdrawn from cultivation. If there are excess resources in the agricultural sector, on the other hand, or if the policy aim is to contract that sector, the tax should be sufficient, in combination with all other tax and expenditure measures, to release resources to the extent and of the type indicated by the development plan. From the standpoint of economic policy the acid test of fiscal adequacy always is the effect upon the allocation and intensity of use of resources. Government officials should be constantly on guard, therefore, against pushing the process of taxing and spending beyond the point of maximum efficiency of resource use.

If it is determined that a land tax will be paid primarily at the expense of the landlord's share, then the level of the tax should be determined in relation to the relative essentiality of the spending or saving that landlords will be unable to do because of the tax. Similarly, if it appears that the tax will be borne primarily by tenants, then the use which tenants would otherwise make of the funds should be the strategic consideration.

Because the effects of taxation on private spending for consumption and investment are not easily measured, these rules cannot be applied with precision. Nevertheless, they can still be helpful to officials seeking to narrow the range of tax yields which would be reasonably consistent with the requirements of economic policy. As already mentioned, the rules — or rather the analytical framework on which they rest — also have implications for the expenditures side of the government's budget. In fact, taxation which encroaches upon private subsistence spending may still be economically sound if it is needed to support relatively more effective government spending on vital public welfare services (for example, health and sanitation).

The Tax Base

In the following analysis of the tax base from the viewpoint of economic policy, attention will be centered upon those economic effects that are associated with the nature of the tax base itself and are independent of the level of the tax, its distributional pattern, and its responsiveness to changes in production and prices. Like many of the earlier analytical distinctions, this one also is artificial, but it is unavoidable if the economic effects are to be evaluated systematically. The criteria for testing the economic effects of the tax base will be the major policy objectives for the agricultural sector, as outlined in the preceding chapter: (1) increased efficiency of production, (2) increased utilization of available resources, (3) desirable resource transfers, and (4) welfare objectives (reduced income disparities, improved living standards, and so on).

The Favorite of Economic Theory

A distinction is often made in theory between income that is economic surplus and income that is a necessary economic reward. A tax on the first class of income has no deterrent effects on production, since the income that is taxed accrues to a *passive* agent. A tax on the second class of income, however, does tend to discourage production, since the income accrues to an *active* agent and is therefore necessary to induce economic activity. This fundamental contrast provides the conceptual foundation for the economic proposition that taxes on surplus income have unique qualifications as ideal revenue measures. A land tax based on pure economic rent, as defined in Ricardian theory, is one of the model taxes in this category.[2]

[2] See Chapter IV, pp. 79–81.

This ideal type of land tax, however, is merely an intellectual creation without any important real-life counterpart. With the exception of "site value," the productive qualities of soil are exhaustible, and any tax on the value of these soil qualities acts as a deterrent to their replenishment. To restrict the tax to the site value of agricultural land – assuming such a restriction to be administratively feasible – would probably condemn it to virtual oblivion as a revenue producer. The rental value taxes found in many parts of the world today fail to satisfy the Ricardian prescription, because the tax bases invariably include a return on the value of capital invested in the land.

On occasion, development projects, such as irrigation or road building, give rise to large increments in land value in the immediate localities benefiting from the projects. Taxing away the value increments by means of "betterment levies" (also known as "special assessments") would have economic advantages of the type ascribed to taxes on surplus income and would probably meet with ready acceptance by the taxpayers, owing to the presence of visible local benefits.[3] Another special circumstance in which the theoretically ideal tax base might find practical, if limited, application is when land values experience a substantial, general advance such as might occur during an inflation. This might be the occasion for an incremental value tax, which would be favored on grounds of equity as well as economic policy, although its revenue potential would probably be small and its application might be hampered by administrative complexities.

Marginal Impact of Taxation

As the "cutting edge" of the tax instrument, the marginal tax rate (i.e., the rate at which the last increment of production or income is taxed) is frequently the focal point of analysis when the economic effects of a tax are at issue. In theory, an individual

[3] Because of its benefit aspect, this type of levy is usually classified as a nontax revenue. See W. J. Shultz and C. L. Harriss, *American Public Finance* (6th ed.; New York, 1954), pp. 469–473. Betterment levies are discussed in Chapter XI.

will be disposed to work harder or to invest more the smaller the tax collector's share of the rewards for additional effort or investment. The force of this theoretical argument, however, fades away when it is applied to the typical farmer whose work habits are determined simply by what needs to be done to enable him to eke out a scanty livelihood, and whose investment is dependent largely on what he can afford to invest and on his capacity to make additional investments pay off. Nevertheless, there are certain types of economic decisions in agriculture that may be influenced by the marginal impact of taxation.

The marginal tax rate is based in part on the rate schedule specified by law. Since land taxes, with few exceptions, are imposed at proportional rates, the statutory rate usually does not vary with the size of the tax base. In addition, the marginal tax rate depends on the definition of the tax base and the frequency of reassessments. Whenever land taxes are assessed according to the productive capacity of the land, as indicated by such factors as soil type, location of field, and availability of irrigation, or according to capital value, which is the price the land could command if offered for sale on the market, the tax base tends to reflect long-run values and to be independent of the actual income which individual cultivators of varying skills and diligence are able to derive from working the land. Moreover, when these values are the result of cadastral surveys, they are unlikely to be revised except after long delays. Thus, by reason of the nature of the tax base and the infrequency of its revision, the tax tends to be a fixed annual charge against the land; for all practical purposes, the marginal tax rate can be assumed to be zero in these cases. As a rule, the zero marginal rate is inadvertent and not a conscious incentive device, although some governments seem to have been acutely aware of the potential stimulus to production offered by a tax plan which leaves the rewards for additional productive effort undiminished by taxation.[4]

[4] Some examples are cited in Walter W. Heller, "The Use of Agricultural Taxation for Incentive Purposes," *Papers and Proceedings of the Conference*

Tithe-like levies and taxes on marketed produce are the only important classes of land taxes which are assessed currently on the basis of actual production or sales; hence, at least in the short run, they are virtually the only land taxes with marginal effective rates greater than zero. Farmers subject to these types of land taxes can ordinarily expect the government to share in their increased output. (By the same token, the government will also share with farmers the burden of a reduction in production.) Of course, the taxes will absorb only a part – and probably a relatively small part – of an increase in output, so that farmers still stand to gain from more intensive productive efforts.

Despite the existence of institutional and human factors which prevent the marginal tax rate as such from having a large economic impact on most farmers, there are a few situations in which the marginal rate may play a crucial economic role. Consider, for example, the case of submarginal land which might be brought into production through reclamation, irrigation, or other means of land development. Taxing the produce of newly reclaimed land would reduce the return to the developers. Where the prospective return (exclusive of tax) was not overly attractive in the first place, the prospective imposition of the tax might be sufficient to deter potential developers. The deterrent effect would of course vary with the size of the tax in the event that the land became productive. Many countries seeking to encourage land development expressly exempt reclaimed land from taxation for a stated number of years; a few countries go further and grant subsidies for land development. Tax administration practices which delay placing rehabilitated land on the tax rolls for several years might serve the same purpose as statutory tax exemption.

Investment other than land reclamation would not appear to be so exposed to the influence of the marginal tax rate. In many cases the assessment formulae look only to the economic value of

---

on Agricultural Taxation and Economic Development (Cambridge, 1954), pp. 223–224.

the land itself, irrespective of improvements on the land (except for such investment as is required to maintain the fertility of the soil). In these cases farmers contemplating new investments need not have any fear of subjecting themselves to increased taxation. Even when the law requires inclusion of the value of improvements in the tax base, there is a high probability that the assessments are behindhand. On the other hand, in those sections where tax assessments are based not upon soil characteristics but upon outward evidences of productive wealth, the prospect of a heavier tax might discourage the acquisition of new wealth. A forcible illustration of this point is provided by the report that concern over taxation induced villagers in some Middle Eastern countries to hide their livestock when government officials arrived to inoculate against rinderpest.[5]

On the whole, the potentially favorable incentive effects of exempting improvements from the tax base would seem to be smaller in agricultural areas than in cities where improvements represent a larger proportion of the tax base. Moreover, business decisions to invest in residential, commercial, and industrial building are likely to be more closely tied to detailed calculations of expected profits than are the investment decisions of a typical farmer.[6] Even so, urban property taxes apply almost universally to the combined value of buildings and land, in apparent disregard of incentive aspects. One possible justification of this policy is that some urban services of government tend to be related to the value of improvements.

Probably more important from an economic standpoint than the policy with respect to taxation of improvements on agricultural land is the policy with respect to taxation of marginal producers. Imposition of a tax on a field which is capable of yielding only a bare subsistence standard will either force the land out of

[5] *Conference on Agricultural Taxation*, p. 26.

[6] The incentive and other arguments for exempting improvements are analyzed in Jens P. Jensen, "Exemption of Improvements," *Tax Exemptions* (Tax Policy League, New York, 1939), pp. 206–221.

production or else so impoverish the cultivator that he cannot possibly become an efficient producer. A farmer barely able to feed and clothe himself and his family is unlikely to be interested in soil conservation and cannot risk experimenting with new techniques of cultivation. Moreover, economic incentives are easily blunted by poverty. All land taxes which fail to provide adequate allowances for production costs (including the risk of crop failures and the cost of transportation to market) are potentially damaging to production for these reasons.

In principle, a tax base tied to a rental value concept should leave marginal producers tax free (since the land they work has no true rental value), but this is not usually the case in practice. The prevailing method is to assess and tax all cultivated fields, even uneconomic holdings, whether a rental value concept or some other base is used, except when such fields are excluded by a minimum exemption.

It should be noted that exempting marginal producers will sometimes result in other producers being taxed more heavily. It seems unlikely, however, that the salutory effect of the exemption on production would be completely offset by a curtailment because of the added tax on other producers.

Effects on Composition of Production

Up to this point, two types of economic effects associated with the nature of the tax base have been singled out as potentially damaging to agricultural output: (1) those effects caused by the impact of the tax on production increments resulting from various forms of new investment; and (2) those effects attributable to the impact of the tax on marginal producers. It was concluded that many land taxes escape censure on the first count, but that most of them are open to serious objection on the second.

The viewpoint of economic policy is also implicated whenever land taxes influence the composition of production. The opportunities for such influence tend to be limited in economies dominated by a single crop or where the land is not readily adaptable to growing other crops. Some diversification in production is almost always present, however, and in many countries growing conditions are favorable to a wide range of crops. Because types of production which may have been suitable to a country many years ago may not be equally suitable today, governmental programs often aim at redirecting agricultural output in the interest of national policy. The goal may be to encourage crops (or other forms of agricultural output) which promise higher returns relative to the input of productive factors, or are a lucrative source of foreign exchange, or are needed to improve national dietary habits. Agricultural experimentation in recent years has disclosed many ways in which changes in land use can bring higher yields.

Almost any type of land tax affords opportunities for favoring certain kinds of agricultural activity and penalizing others. The opportunities are most easily exploited when the tax rate or method of taxation varies according to the kinds of activity; in South Korea, for example, staple foods are taxed under a rate schedule different from that for garden vegetables and orchard fruits, and in Libya cereals are subject to a tithe-like levy while vegetable gardens are assessed on the basis of area. In other cases, especially when the tax base is intended to reflect the productive capacity of the land, the assessment formula frequently employs official prices, as opposed to actual market prices, in valuing output; determination of the official prices presents a ready means of deliberately differentiating according to types of crops. In addition, more favorable taxation of some products may result simply from peculiarities of the assessment methods.

For a tax to be neutral in its effects on the composition of production, it should exact the same proportion of net income from each product, thereby leaving undisturbed the relative attractiveness of different productive activities. When a tax exacts unequal proportions, it tends to encourage farmers to shift to the more lightly taxed products. It is of course impossible to specify how sizable the tax differentials must be before such shifts will actually occur, although some indication might be obtained from field studies of tax effects in specific countries. With gross production or land area as the tax base, the tax may represent considerably different proportions of net income for crops that require relatively large outlays for seed, fertilizer, irrigation, and hired labor than for crops that are more easily cultivated, and the resulting differentials might be large enough to induce some shift of production. Marketing taxes also fall with uneven weight on net earnings from different kinds of output. Rental value taxes, based on either annual rental value or capital value, probably are more nearly neutral than most other types, since the rental value base at least allows for differences in the productive capacity of land. In each case, however, the effects depend more on how the tax is actually administered than on the formal definition of the tax base.

It should be noted that impartiality among the different agricultural products is not necessarily the preferred goal. Agricultural policy may indicate a need for taxes which penalize certain producers and give relatively favorable treatment to others, and an alert officialdom will attempt to meet that need. It would be rash, therefore, to condemn all taxes that affect the composition of production; the tax-induced changes in production may sometimes serve national policy, even though the taxes were not enacted with that purpose in mind.

Effects on Volume of Marketings

An increased volume of agricultural marketings often is a vital policy goal, especially in rapidly developing economies. Such an increase may be needed to support growing consumption requirements in urban areas, to expand exports, or to displace imports; at the same time, the proceeds of larger marketings may permit farmers to improve their own living standards or to acquire new productive equipment.

Those small-scale producers who are largely outside the

money economy may be induced to bring more of their product to the market if their commitments for cash tax payments are increased. Otherwise, the chief impact of land taxation on the proportion of output made available to the nonagricultural sector is through the differential effect of taxation on the proportion marketed and the proportion retained for the farmer's own use. A marketing tax exerts that type of differential effect and for that reason may be considered a deterrent to the marketing of products.

The average cultivator producing primarily for commercial markets, however, is not likely to be deterred by a marketing tax, even though the rate is as high as, say, 12½ per cent (which is the rate recently in effect in Iraq). His livelihood depends upon how much he is able to produce and sell, and the imposition of a tax on his sales is as likely to spur him to work harder as it is to deter him. Nevertheless, as under any form of tax which does not exempt marginal producers, a marketing tax might force marginal farms out of production.

The more seriously deterrent effects of marketing taxes are on farmers who are not primarily market-oriented and therefore need to be given every possible inducement to bring their products to the market place. Farmers who are distant from distribution centers may be in that situation, and if the prices their products bring in the market are reduced by taxation, they may stop sending their products. The force of this objection to marketing taxes will, of course, vary with the particular conditions of agriculture in each country.

The Distributional Pattern

The equity aspects of the distributional patterns of different taxes were considered in an earlier chapter; there are economic aspects of the patterns which should also be assessed. In the first place, the extent to which taxation affects the allocation of production between consumption and investment is partly dependent on its distributional pattern. Taxes collected from low-income farmers usually represent funds which would otherwise have been used for consumption, since these farmers ordinarily are unable to do much saving. Taxes collected from wealthier groups may be at the expense of reduced consumption or reduced saving. Saving takes many forms, and when it is curtailed by taxation the result may be smaller hoards of cash and precious jewels, or it may be lower outlays for improvements on the land or for new equipment.

The risk that essential investment will be curtailed because taxes on upper income groups will absorb necessary funds does not seem to be a serious one in many underdeveloped countries, where much of the private investment in agriculture does not require large cash outlays and where institutional factors and a tendency to resist technological changes are the chief obstacles to increased private investment. In any country where agricultural investment is closely dependent on the availability of funds, however, the distributional pattern should be planned so that the taxation of funds destined for investment is held to a minimum, or else other action should be taken to relieve the problem of financing investment. Relatively heavy taxes on high-income cultivators and landlords will probably less often absorb funds needed for investment than funds that would otherwise be spent for luxuries or accumulate as idle savings. When that is the case, concern over the effects of the taxes on savings and investment need not act as a restraint upon the progressiveness of the tax system in the agricultural sector.

The distributional pattern of land taxation is likely to be of more decisive importance because of its effects on living standards and income inequalities than because of its effect on the volume of private investment. In many countries there are large rural populations barely subsisting on annual incomes (cash and noncash) as low as $25 and $50 per capita. As already indicated, to lift these people out of their poverty is more than a humanitarian goal; it is also an economic necessity, because poverty gives rise to much waste of manpower and productive talent. These practical considerations underscore the previous arguments in favor of a distributional pattern which exempts from taxation families at the very bottom of the income scale, or otherwise taxes them lightly in comparison with the taxes paid by the rest of the population.

As noted above, very few land taxes include a basic minimum exemption. Marketing taxes are something of an exception by virtue of the fact that they do not apply to products retained by the farmer for his own use. However, farmers who do not grow basic foods but instead such products as tobacco gain little advantage from the exemption of home consumption under a marketing tax.

Moreover, for most types of land taxes the distributional pattern probably is regressive, so that the proportion of net income absorbed by the taxes declines as income increases. This is generally true, for example, when the tax base is gross production – assuming that the tax rate is proportional and not graduated – because of the failure of the base to include allowances for differences in unit costs of production. Fields producing the same gross harvests may yield substantially different net incomes. The pattern need not be regressive when the base is annual rental value or capital value, but under prevailing administrative practices wealthy farmers generally seem to fare relatively better with the tax assessors than do taxpayers who are financially less well-off. When properly assessed, rental value or capital value taxes distinguish between high-cost and low-cost productive units by making allowances for cost differentials attributable to the qualities of the soil, availability of irrigation, climate, accessibility to markets, and other factors affecting land value. These taxes, however, do not allow for net income differences traceable to the cultivator's skill and diligence.

The more regressive the distributional pattern, the larger the relative impact of the tax on essential consumption and the smaller its impact on luxury consumption. In addition, a regressive pattern tends to widen existing income inequalities. Most countries would probably prefer to avoid such effects and instead to distribute taxes so that they are paid primarily at the expense of nonessential consumption and uninvested savings. To achieve these results may require both a minimum exemption (varying with the number of the taxpayer's dependents) and a tax base that represents a constant or a rising proportion of net income at successively higher income levels. The appropriateness of graduated tax rates also needs to be considered.

In countries which have had an equalizing of agricultural incomes — probably as a result of a land reform — these distributional issues may recede in importance.

Structural Flexibility

The term "structural flexibility" refers to the automatic variation of tax collections with changes in prices and production, the variation having its source in the structure and administration of the tax rather than in deliberate adjustments in the tax rates or exemptions. As described in Chapter II, most land taxes — marketing taxes and tithe-like levies are the exceptions — are conspicuously inflexible, chiefly because they are not subject to annual reassessments.[7] Long-run increases in the value of agricultural production, due either to real growth in output or to a price advance, bring only a slow, delayed response in the yield of these taxes. Should the increases in output or prices last no longer than a year or two, the tax yield is unlikely to respond at all (except insofar as an improvement in agricultural incomes will reduce tax delinquency rates).

Recent experience is replete with examples of land taxes which have lost their former dominance as revenue producers because of their failure to keep pace with an inflation or a rapid

[7] Collections in kind instead of in cash assure revenue flexibility with respect to changes in prices; see the section that follows.

expansion of output.[8] There are many examples, too, of countries in which a temporary spurt in agricultural income was dissipated in extravagant spending and inflationary price rises. Had these countries been equipped with more flexible revenue instruments, they would have been better able to drain off the excess spending power in order to promote economic stability and more rapid growth.

Flexible taxes are a stabilizing force in any economy exposed to destabilizing influences originating internally or abroad. If an increase in the over-all level of money income brings an increase in tax collections, there is less likelihood that the income expansion will lead to a disruptive inflation; similarly, if a decrease in the over-all level of money income is cushioned by a decrease in tax collections, the chances of averting a deep recession will be enhanced.

Flexible taxes might also play a pivotal role in financing a country's development program. In many countries in the early stages of development, the agricultural sector holds the promise of substantial expansion. The incremental capital-output ratio (i.e., the amount of investment needed per unit of additional output) tends to be lower in agriculture than in industry, and the returns usually come more quickly. A sustained, rapid pace of development will be difficult to achieve, however, unless part of the increase in agricultural income is captured by appropriately flexible revenue instruments and the proceeds used for financing additional investment in agriculture or in the industrial sector. Otherwise, most of the increase will be consumed.

Not all of the economic arguments favor flexibility, however. Earlier in this chapter it was shown that stable taxes — with a zero marginal rate — avoid interfering with work and investment incentives. Due regard must therefore be given to the possibly adverse effects of a flexible tax on production. Such effects will not arise if the desired flexibility is achieved through frequent

[8] See above, pp. 54–55, 63.

over-all adjustments in the level of assessments rather than through individual adjustments according to each taxpayer's output that year. Moreover, the main area of possible conflict between the objective of flexibility and the desire for optimum incentive arrangements can usually be eliminated merely by granting tax exemption to production attributable to new investment. Such an exemption need not materially weaken the effectiveness of revenue flexibility as a stabilizing force, and it would of course help to encourage more rapid agricultural development.

The fact that receipts from marketing taxes and tithe-like levies on gross production automatically respond to changes in the value of output is an important economic consideration in their favor. It would seem, however, that the barriers to introducing substantial flexibility into other forms of taxing land produce and income are not hard to overcome.[9]

Collections in Kind

In some of the less developed countries – notably, mainland China, South Korea, and Taiwan – land taxes are collected in kind instead of in cash.[10] The method of in-kind collections has lost many of its original attractions in most areas of the world, because of the fact that agriculture is not so completely outside

[9] Specific suggestions are offered in Chapter X (see pp. 202–205) below.

[10] Burma's State Agricultural Marketing Board may be viewed as an instrument for taxation in kind. A recent study by Jonathan Levin ("A Theory of Export Economies," unpublished doctoral dissertation, Fletcher School of Law and Diplomacy, April, 1956) describes the SAMB as "the Government's main instrument for taxing the farmer" (p. 207). Not all of SAMB's profits can be considered a tax on agriculturalists; part represents income which previously accrued to foreign traders.

The Soviet Union makes extensive use of a special form of taxation in kind in the agricultural sector. Collective farms and individual peasants are required to deliver a specified portion of their output to the state for a remuneration that is considerably below the market value. The difference between the cost (procurement price plus processing and distribution costs) and the selling price is siphoned into the state budget by the turnover tax. The portion of the turnover tax which is collected by virtue of the low pro-the monetary economy as formerly. For the most part, countries currently making extensive use of in-kind collections do so primarily because the system offers special advantages over cash collections as an instrument of economic policy — especially as applied to food distribution — under the exceptional conditions prevailing in these countries.

Whether collections are in kind or in cash need not affect the basic structure of the land tax. Hence, what has already been said about the economic implications of the tax base, distributional pattern, and flexibility is generally applicable to both in-kind and cash taxes. Nevertheless, the economic effects of the two types of taxes offer some significant contrasts.

In the first place, in-kind taxes probably open up more opportunities than cash taxes for influences on the composition of production. A government may wish to avail itself of these opportunities, provided that it can reasonably expect agricultural producers to respond to tax inducements. One such opportunity arises out of the employment of equivalency ratios between different crops; these ratios give farmers the option of paying their taxes with any one of several basic crops. Should the equivalency ratios stay fixed over a long period, the advantages of paying with one crop rather than another will shift with changing price relationships. Furthermore, the government is able to accept in-kind payments in only a limited number of staple crops, usually grains. Thus, producers of, say, vegetables or fruits must be permitted to pay in cash, or else their tax liability must be expressed in terms of a basic crop even though their harvest consists of other products. Whenever the resulting tax differentials among farmers fail to correspond with differences in net

---

curement price is partly land rent and partly the monetary equivalent of the tax in kind. According to F. D. Holzman, *Soviet Taxation* (Cambridge: Harvard University Press, 1955), p. 84: "A crucial feature of the tax in kind . . . is that it is based on the number of acres sown or owned rather than on actual output"; see also pp. 82–86, 159–176. Compulsory deliveries at below-market prices have a long history as a fiscal instrument in many countries of Eastern Europe and Asia.

income, farmers are given an inducement to produce the more lightly taxed commodities and to refrain from producing those that are relatively heavily taxed.

Secondly, in-kind collections appear to offer advantages over cash collections when the government has set a very high revenue goal for the land tax. According to the statistics cited in Chapter III, mainland China and Korea head the list when countries are ranked according to the relative importance of land taxes in their revenue systems. Moreover, the proportion of the total grain harvest absorbed by the in-kind taxes – approximately one-third in China and more than one-tenth in Korea – provides a particularly striking comparison with the much smaller proportions in countries with cash taxes.[11]

The most plausible explanation of the comparatively high yields of the in-kind taxes would seem to be that such taxes are not limited by the availability of cash resources in the agricultural sector; thus a tax contribution can be obtained even from very small producers who customarily restrict themselves to barter transactions and do not market crops for cash. For that reason China and Korea – countries where the bulk of agricultural output is produced by farmers earning very low incomes – would find it difficult to maintain the currently high yields of their land taxes if they shifted to cash collections. A contributing explanation for the high yields may be that the countries with in-kind taxes are in a stronger position, for political and institutional reasons, than are most other countries to impose relatively heavy fiscal burdens on the agricultural population.

The income from in-kind taxes includes more than the tax yield alone; it also includes some profits which would otherwise accrue to private distributors of agricultural commodities. When the government collects grain from farmers, stores it, and later moves it into wholesale or retail trade channels or distributes it in other ways, the government is performing the middleman's

[11] See above, pp. 62, 64–65. Comparable statistics are not at hand for Taiwan.

functions and carrying his risks. It would be difficult to compute the government's compensation for these services separately from the tax yield itself, unless the computation were made merely by assuming a certain percentage mark-up. The net receipts (taxes and profits combined) from the in-kind collections represent the difference between the aggregate market value of the commodities when they are distributed and the total cost of storage, transportation, and distribution.[12] When governments reserve part of the collections for the military services and relief activities, they will customarily credit the tax receipts with the value of the commodities so distributed.

Thirdly, in-kind taxes have a distinct superiority over cash taxes when a country is experiencing inflation. Cash holdings depreciate in value as prices rise, but inventories of goods retain their value. In-kind taxes thus provide the treasury with a kind of insurance against loss of purchasing power of its tax receipts in the event that prices rise; by reducing the need for deficit financing, such taxes are more effective than cash taxes in combating inflation. Should prices fall, however, the treasury would be better off holding cash instead of goods; on the other hand, it can be argued that in-kind taxes help to stabilize prices and income in a depression because they do not reduce private spending to the same extent that cash taxes do.

Finally, in-kind taxes represent a convenient means for the government to acquire a sizable portion of each harvest and thereby exert some control over the distribution and prices of agricultural products. This consideration seems to have been of paramount importance in South Korea, for example, where the in-kind tax has served as a key instrument of national food policy and has also been important in the government's effort to control prices and wage rates. In 1951, when the tax was introduced, the

[12] A common practice is to understate the tax yield by valuing the commodities at official prices, which are below market prices. For a discussion of the method of valuation of grain collections in Korea, see Haskell P. Wald, "Use of Tax Collections in Kind to Combat Inflation in the Republic of Korea," *Public Finance*, vol. IX, no. 2, pp. 184–185.

government of South Korea was committed to purchasing huge quantities of rice — by far the country's largest staple crop — for distribution to the army, national police, government employees, and the sizable relief population. Workers in industry also were receiving a rice supplement as part of their wage; because of the inflation, this supplement gave workers many of the benefits of an escalator clause in their wage contracts. Because of difficulties in acquiring the necessary quantities of rice, the government had fallen behind in its rice distributions in 1951, and a large part of the population faced serious hardship as a result. The substitution of in-kind for money taxes eased many of the government's problems with respect to food distribution and wage-price control.[13]

When agricultural taxes are paid in kind, the government must establish a type of business agency to take charge of the commodities that are paid in. The agency may restrict its activities largely to storage, in which case the commodities would be returned to regular distribution channels as soon as selling opportunities arise; or the agency may also control the distribution by supplying the requirements of the army and other government programs for agricultural commodities, while distributing the remainder of the collections through private wholesale or retail outlets or government stores (including relief centers), and perhaps through exports. Through its control over a sizable portion of the food supply outside the agricultural sector, the agency may also seek to regulate food prices. As far as can be determined, the government's desire to obtain more effective control over both food distribution and commodity prices was a primary motivating factor in most of the recent cases of increased reliance on in-kind taxes.[14]

[13] The Korean experience is described in Haskell P. Wald, "The Recent Experience of the Republic of Korea with Tax Collections in Kind," *Conference on Agricultural Taxation*, pp. 424–431.

[14] Holzman observes that the Soviet Union's tax in kind "gives the state the direct control over agricultural output necessary for the Soviet brand of planning in a sector of the economy which is not formally state owned" (p.

Summary and Conclusions

This chapter has sought to interpret the viewpoint of economic policy in terms of the broad goals of agricultural development and to single out the specific policy areas where the method of land taxation seems directly relevant to a country's success in reaching these goals. Because it is not possible to make a categorical appraisal of each method of taxation from the standpoint of its compliance with the full set of economic policy criteria, the chapter merely lays down certain principles for the general guidance of tax policy officials. The main principles may be summarized as follows:

1. The economically optimum level of land taxation should be decided ultimately on the basis of the effects on the allocation and intensity of use of resources. The basic objective is to absorb by taxation that amount of purchasing power which can be diverted with economic advantage from private hands to the government.

2. The marginal impact of taxation on production and investment should be softened by providing exemptions which encourage land reclamation and improvements on the land.

3. To the extent feasible, marginal producers should be tax-free; otherwise they will be prevented from becoming more efficient producers and they may even be forced out of production entirely.

4. Tax differentials which favor certain types of agricultural production over other types should be avoided, except when the

86). It is interesting to note that a journalist covering the war in Indo-China in 1954 reported that the rice tax proved to be a "marvelously efficient" means of feeding and paying the soldiers during the fighting (Joseph Alsop, in New York *Herald Tribune*, December 27, 1954, p. 10). Burma's SAMB has a broader orientation than its counterparts in most other countries, since it is an integral part of a larger government program for the promotion of the welfare of cultivators and for the stabilization of prices at the farm and at retail (Levin, pp. 204–208).

differences in tax treatment are clearly in accord with development objectives.

5. Taxes which fall more heavily on the portion of the harvest that is marketed than on the portion retained on the farm may impede desirable resource transfers because of their tendency to discourage agricultural marketings.

6. Taxes should be distributed so that low-income families are taxed lightly, if at all; to tax them relatively heavily would impinge upon their essential consumption requirements and magnify existing income inequalities.

7. Taxes should vary with changes in production and prices in order to contribute to the country's economic stability and to permit diverting part of the increase in income, as the economy expands, to development financing.

8. Tax collections in kind can be a powerful instrument of economic policy, especially when the government is interested in obtaining increased control over food distribution and food prices.

In view of the close dependence of the economic effects of land taxes on the actual conditions in the countries where the taxes are imposed, expert discretion is necessary for the correct application of these principles. While the principles are believed to have wide application in the less developed countries, they obviously do not all deserve the same emphasis everywhere. Some of the principles may ultimately be ruled out on grounds of equity or administrative feasibility — or possibly because they conflict with other economic objectives — but others can be put into practice in the expectation that the drive for economic development will thereby be benefited.

IX

THE VIEWPOINT OF ADMINISTRATION

AMONG THE family of considerations bearing upon tax policy, the viewpoint of administration is in many ways the easiest one to interpret, though application of sound administrative principles may be very difficult. Whereas the equity and economic effects of taxation often are uncertain and difficult to evaluate, the administrative results are in plain sight and to a large extent allow direct measurement. The government's cost of tax collection can be expressed as a monetary expense, and the over-all extent of tax evasion – which is an important index of administrative performance – can usually be determined with a reasonable degree of accuracy. Only in the case of compliance costs – which comprise the tangible and intangible expenses borne by the taxpayers in meeting the tax laws – is it generally necessary to fall back upon rough approximations.

Simply as a matter of expediency, makers of tax policy cannot avoid considering the viewpoint of administration from the very start of their deliberations. Tax proposals which are clearly beyond the government's capacity to administer with reasonable efficiency can be immediately rejected. Other proposals which would place that capacity under heavy strain can be ruled out, unless they have compelling, nonadministrative advantages which may be attainable despite the troublesome problems of administration. Tax planning, however, should allow for the expected growth of a country's administrative capacity to undertake more advanced methods of taxation, and of its capacity to bear the heavier cost of these methods as the country achieves economic progress.

The policy makers' golden dream is to find a tax that combines administrative simplicity and economy with a full measure of the other virtues of an ideal levy. Because tax collection and compliance costs represent a use of resources, there is a needless economic waste when these costs are unnecessarily high. It would, however, be mistaken to assume that success in applying the viewpoint of administration always requires holding administrative costs to the absolute minimum in relation to the revenue yield; a more constructive approach is to seek a proper balance between administrative costs and other objectives of tax policy. While much can be said in favor of simple, readily administered taxes, such taxes do not always serve a country's long-run interests. For example, correction of tax inequities or elimination of undesirable tax effects may necessitate provisions that will entail added administrative cost without a commensurate gain in revenue.

The purpose of the present chapter is, first, to investigate the principal factors bearing upon the relative ease or difficulty of administering land taxes in countries in the early stages of economic development, and second, to indicate the nature of the administrative requirements for the principal types of land taxes.

Foundations of Successful Administration

Just as taxes differ widely in their administrative requirements, so do governments differ in their respective capabilities for tax administration. To a great extent, success in tax administration goes hand-in-hand with success in other branches of government administration. A government that is plagued with inefficiency in various of its operations will ordinarily be inefficient in tax administration, no matter how simply the tax system is designed. On the other hand, a government that has achieved a generally high administrative standard in the conduct of its affairs is in a strong position to duplicate that standard in tax administration, even when relatively complex levies are involved. Although tax administration often raises problems which are not present in other branches of government, many administrative techniques are transferable among the different branches. This does not mean, however, that improvement in tax administration cannot be accomplished in advance of general administrative reforms; indeed, if a promising start is made in improving tax administration, many of the reforms can be carried over to other branches of government.

Though many factors determine a government's ability to administer taxes efficiently, two factors of far-reaching importance might be singled out here for special mention: (1) the quality of the administrative personnel and (2) the national attitude toward the tax system.[1]

Most of the less developed countries face serious handicaps in recruiting an adequate and reliable staff of competent officials for tax administration. There may be an actual shortage of qualified persons in the country, as a result of inadequate training facilities and low educational standards. All too often pay scales and working conditions are so poor as to discourage competent persons from entering the public service. On occasion the underlying difficulty is governmental inability to wipe out corruption among its employees and to correct a system of political favoritism that prevents impartial treatment of taxpayers.

Problems of personnel are especially likely to beset land tax administration. Most land taxes require a large decentralized staff located in farming communities all over the country. Not only is it extremely difficult to recruit qualified persons for assignment in rural areas, where living conditions are usually poor and few local residents can qualify as tax officials because educational opportunities are so limited; but it is also practically impossible to maintain close supervision over the field staff under

[1] These and other aspects of tax administration are reviewed in Stanley S. Surrey, "Tax Administration in Underdeveloped Countries," paper presented at Meeting of International Institute of Public Finance, Rio de Janeiro, 1954; reprinted, 1958, in *U. of Miami Law Review*, XII, no. 2, pp. 158–188.

such circumstances. Moreover, land taxes are usually collected at harvest time, which means that the work load is highly seasonal. This fact often encourages reliance upon part-time officials who are unlikely to be subject to the same hiring standards and discipline as are career public servants.[2]

Where the quality of the tax staff is unsatisfactory, governments should give highest priority to its improvement by organizing a more effective recruitment program, instituting appropriate training procedures, and weeding out inefficient or dishonest employees. Pending substantial accomplishment along such lines, a government would probably do well to favor those forms of taxation that are relatively least demanding in their administrative requirements. It should be emphasized, however, that simplification of the tax system is never a satisfactory substitute for building a strong, capable corps of tax administrators.

The relative effectiveness of tax administration also depends largely upon the national attitude toward the tax system. Willing taxpayer compliance will ease the task of tax collection and enforcement in many important ways and will produce substantial savings in administrative costs. Such steps as clarifying the rules and regulations and conducting extensive educational campaigns to explain the tax laws and the individual taxpayer's responsibilities can help to create a co-operative attitude among taxpayers. In the final analysis, however, willing compliance is unlikely unless the public has considerable confidence in the government itself, as well as in the basic equitableness of the tax system, the fairness with which taxes are assessed and collected, and the manner in which government funds are handled.[3] There doubtless are many countries today where tax administration is being

[2] In India, except in areas under permanent settlement, there is a well-organized system of village officials who actually collect the land revenue, prepare accounts, and keep records. Until recently, most of these officials held their posts on a hereditary basis. See *Report of the Taxation Enquiry Commission, 1953–54* (Government of India, 1955), III, 187–188.

[3] A policy of setting aside a portion of the taxes collected in a local area for expenditure there often helps to build public support for payment of taxes.

frustrated more by the public's lack of confidence in the government's fiscal management than by any other single factor.

Land Administration as an Aid to Tax Administration

Many of the basic administrative requirements of land taxation can be satisfied in conjunction with the government's administration of a land program. It is not surprising, therefore, to find that the better administered land taxes are generally found in countries with well-developed systems of land administration.[4]

The major fields of land administration include: (1) registration of property rights, including water rights and rights to forests and grazing land; (2) supervision of the land tenure system, including terms of leasing agreements, rights of leaseholders, and rights of secondary occupation; and (3) preparation of an inventory of land resources, including mapping of public and private lands and surveys of soil productivity and land use.

Land administration can be most helpful in connection with two phases of land tax administration: property identification and property valuation. The main instrument of a successful system of land administration is the cadastre, which is the official record of the location, size, and ownership (or other basis of occupancy) of each tract of land in the area covered.[5] Thus, a properly executed cadastre that is kept up to date will provide the land tax officials with information on the exact location of each field, its size, shape, and topographical features, the owner's name, and the names of tenants (if any). In addition, the cadastre may record much information regarding the sale or rental value of the field and the crops produced. Land may be classified in the cadastre according to such factors as (1) soil types (texture,

[4] Land administration has been developed most systematically in the Indo-Pakistan subcontinent and the Far East, where land taxes have had their greatest success. The heavy investment of these countries in cadastral records provides a weighty argument for continued use of land taxes as a major revenue source.

[5] For a description of cadastral surveys, see above, pp. 46–50.

permeability, thickness of surface soil, moisture-holding capacity, chemical characteristics, etc.), (2) present use (cropland by types of crops grown, pastureland, orchards, timberland, etc.), and (3) use capabilities (i.e., capacity for producing various crops).[6] Additional sources of aid to property valuation for tax purposes are present when the land administration records include such data as sales prices at time of transfer, rental fees, and statistics on actual production for each field.

Land administration has acquired new significance in many countries in recent years because of increased emphasis upon agricultural credit programs, land conservation, promotion of better land use, and improvement of tenancy conditions.[7] Moreover, accurate land records are valuable for the carrying out of a land reform involving changes in existing rights in land.

The experience throughout most of Latin America, where land administration is generally in a primitive stage – to the extent that some countries do not even have an adequate system of title registration – provides a convincing demonstration of the tendency for taxes that are tied to land ownership or income in the agricultural sector to remain crude and relatively ineffective as revenue producers until the country develops a satisfactory system of land administration.[8] Accomplishment of the latter objective will still leave many problems of land taxation unsolved, but it will at least lay the groundwork for a vastly improved and more productive system of land taxation.

[6] In recent years soil classification methods have been perfected to the point where the permissible range of soil characteristics within a soil type or phase is sufficiently narrow to permit reliable predictions as to productivity. See A. R. Aandahl, W. G. Murray, and W. Scholtes, "Economic Rating of Soils for Tax Assessment," *Journal of Farm Economics* (August 1954), pp. 483–489.

[7] See *Cadastral Surveys and Records of Rights in Land,* Food and Agriculture Administration of the United Nations (Rome, March 1953).

[8] For example, see reports of technical assistance missions to Bolivia, Colombia, and Nicaragua, as summarized in *Taxes and Fiscal Policy in Underdeveloped Countries,* United Nations Technical Assistance Administration (New York, 1954), pp. 47–48, 59–62, 96–97. According to Richard Goode, the chief problem in most Latin American countries is not their in-

Influence of Form of Tax on Administrative Requirements

The administrative requirements of a tax are determined, first of all, by various aspects of the local setting. In the case of land taxes, the following local factors would seem to be directly relevant: the land tenure structure, the nature of existing land records, the typical scale of production, the average size of plots, the variety of products, the extent to which agriculture is market-oriented, the scope of the monetary sector, the marketing and distribution system, and the proportion of output exported. For the most part the policy makers can do little to reduce the requirements of tax administration by changing these local factors (except that they can lend their support to basic improvements in land administration, as noted below). They must concentrate their efforts on designing taxes that are appropriate for the local setting and do not create administrative requirements which will prove unduly burdensome.

This section interprets the viewpoint of administration as applied to those provisions of land taxes which affect (1) the government's administrative costs, (2) the taxpayers' compliance burden, and (3) the completeness of collection.[9]

Cost of Administration

Perhaps the most obvious single factor determining the government's costs of tax administration is the number of taxpayers. Broadening the coverage of a tax will almost certainly add to the administrative cost, while narrowing the coverage should permit

---

ability to establish an effective system of title registration and to undertake land surveys, but rather the fact that "intensive use of the property tax is blocked . . . by a small but politically powerful group of large landowners" ("Reconstruction of Foreign Tax Systems," National Tax Association, *Proceedings of Forty-Fourth Annual Conference,* 1951, p. 220).

[9] Many of the provisions examined in this section are relevant to all forms of taxation, not simply to land taxes. See, for example, the discussion of the factors affecting tax administration in the United States in Roy Blough, *The Federal Taxing Process* (New York, 1952), pp. 427–440.

cost savings. In all countries there probably is a cut-off point, established by law or administrative practice, which serves to exclude very small taxpayers; otherwise a disproportionate share of the revenue would be spent in collecting extremely small amounts from these taxpayers. The exemption level, however, may not be determined simply by administrative costs but rather by equity or revenue considerations, or possibly by such administrative factors as the limited size of the tax staff.

The number of taxpayers can be changed not only by adjusting the minimum exemption, but also by shifting the point of collection or the point where the ultimate liability rests. Where there is plantation agriculture, a tax on the owners would involve a comparatively small number of taxpayers. Where tenant farming is prevalent, the number of taxpayers can be reduced by imposing the tax directly upon the landlords rather than upon individual tenants. In a populous country of owner-cultivators, a tax collected when the produce moves to the market probably would involve fewer taxpayers than one collected at the farm. In tribal societies it might be expeditious to levy a collective assessment on each tribal unit.

A second cost factor is the assessment procedure. At one extreme are assessments according to land area, with a minimum number of land classifications; these are probably the least costly to administer satisfactorily. At the other extreme are assessments according to the economic value of the land, expressed as rental or capital value. There are many degrees of possible refinement in the calculation of economic value, but the administrative requirement is appreciable even for a rudimentary value calculation, unless, as sometimes appears to be the case, the country is willing to accept poor fiscal results. If not for the fact that information on land productivity and value is often needed for purposes other than taxation and is therefore included in existing land administration records, the cost of many of today's better adminstered rental value and capital value taxes would be far out of line with that of other taxes. In some countries, however, the expenditure upon land valuation for tax purposes is small because no serious effort is made to value the land properly; this appears to be true in some parts of Latin America, for example, where there are glaring inadequacies in the assessment practices.

When a country's cadastral records include an adequate system of land classification, it is plainly advantageous to tie the tax assessments to that classification. The cadastral records can be most helpful when they are based upon objective criteria and leave little room for administrative discretion. As suggested earlier in this chapter, improvement of land records usually is the most promising means of obtaining a better system of land taxation. On occasion, the interest of the tax assessors has provided the impetus for improved land records. In Germany, for example, it is reported that "the Ministry of Finance was instrumental in perfecting land survey and title recording systems, and in the development of a system of land classification that has been a major contribution in standardizing taxes and rental rates, and in the regulation of the sale of farm land." [10]

Cost calculations necessarily influence decisions regarding what degree of refinement to seek in classifying land for tax purposes. Where the prevailing classification system recognizes only gross variations in land value, the cost of introducing a more discriminating system would be a worthwhile investment for nontax as well as tax reasons. There are certain types of refinements, however, such as those which reflect changing economic factors, which may permit more equitable taxation but may be considered too costly because they do not yield complementary advantages for revenue collection alone or for land administration programs. Starting from the premise that the higher the tax yield, the better the case for more accurate classification methods, the policy makers must seek to balance the estimated additional cost of im-

[10] Philip M. Raup, "Agricultural Taxation and Land Tenure Reform in Underdeveloped Countries," *Papers and Proceedings of the Conference on Agricultural Taxation and Economic Development* (Cambridge, 1954), p. 258.

proved methods against their own assessment of the equity aspects. Provided there are no technical obstacles to introducing more refinements of classification, policy makers are likely to find that their decisions ultimately rest upon intuitive judgments and political considerations, though they may be formed with the aid of as many facts as can be assembled.

Many Latin American countries economize on administrative costs by levying assessments according to whatever information is available on selling prices of farm land, rather than on the basis of land classification surveys. This approach can hardly be expected to produce satisfactory results, however, partly because land is not a commodity which is freely traded in impersonal markets.[11] To rely upon taxpayers' declarations of the value of their holdings obviously is open to even more fundamental objections. Sales data are widely used as the basis for property tax assessments in the United States, although in recent years some communities in farm sections of the United States have stopped relying upon such data and have begun to use soil maps and economic ratings based upon the prospective yield of the land under good management.[12]

When assessments are based upon the volume of production of each field, two alternative assessment procedures exist: on-the-spot inspections by field teams or local officials at harvest time, or derivation of "normal production" for each field according to actual experience in a prior period or on the basis of soil classification surveys. Both of these approaches would seem to be relatively expensive to carry out, except that the second approach need not be costly in those countries having land records that provide the necessary information.

The desire to reduce administrative costs has given strong

[11] See above, pp. 24ff.

[12] A parallel development is taking place in many urban areas where properties are being reassessed by professional appraisers on the basis of physical criteria (type of construction, age of buildings, cubic contents, frontage and depth of lots, etc.) and less reliance is being placed upon sales information.

encouragement to the practice of keeping land tax assessments unchanged for long periods, although it is also true that more frequent reassessments are sometimes prevented by the lack of trained surveyors and soil experts needed for land surveys. Apart from saving the cost of resurveys, a stable assessment simplifies the administrative procedures in such obvious ways as by making it unnecessary to recalculate each taxpayer's liability and by reducing the occasion for taxpayers' appeals.

The cost of land tax administration is also affected by various other tax provisions, such as: (1) the presence of provisions which lead to controversy because they are difficult to interpret and apply; (2) the nature of procedures for granting tax relief and exemptions; (3) the frequency of tax collection and method of enforcing payment; and (4) the extent of co-ordination between tax administration and other government programs (e.g., loan programs, fertilizer distribution, grain collection, rent control).

Compliance Burden

The cost of taxpayer compliance is much less important for most types of land taxes than for other kinds of taxes. Under the typical land tax there are no record-keeping requirements for taxpayers and no tax returns for them to file. In most phases of land tax administration the initiative rests with the tax officials. This statement does not apply, however, to those marketing taxes which are enforced with the aid of detailed accounting records kept by traders operating under the close supervision of government agents.

Some provisions that would reduce the government's cost of land tax administration will also reduce taxpayers' compliance costs. For example, when the assessment standards are easy to interpret and apply, the government's job is simplified and there is less likelihood of the taxpayer disputing his tax bill. In some instances, however, by spending more on administration the government can lighten the taxpayers' compliance burden. This might happen, for example, if the government increased the number of local offices where payments might be made and where appeals for adjustment of assessments might be adjudicated.

Another aspect of the compliance burden is related to the size of the tax. The heavier the tax, the more interested the taxpayer will become in finding ways of reducing his liability. As the tax rate is raised, it therefore becomes more important to close any avenues of escape and also to simplify and standardize tax relief provisions, including any special arrangements for hardship cases. For example, instead of requiring each taxpayer to apply for remission when he believes that he is eligible, it might be preferable to grant automatic relief to groups of taxpayers on the basis of some general criteria. A poor growing season, or a sharp price decline, might provide the occasion for granting such relief.[13]

Completeness of Collection

Holding underpayment of taxes to the lowest practical minimum is the third principal area of concern of tax administration. The consequences of widespread underpayment can be fiscally disastrous not only because of the revenue loss but also because of the damage to the equitableness of the tax and to taxpayer morale.

Under a tax that is assessed by administrative officials and is not dependent upon taxpayers' returns, the completeness of collection depends largely upon the ability of the officials to (1) locate the taxpayers, (2) determine with accuracy each person's liability, and (3) enforce collection by being able and ready to penalize those who fail or refuse to pay. Whether the form of the tax will assist or obstruct the exercise of these administrative functions is sometimes an important policy consideration.

In any country which has a full set of cadastral maps and complete land registers, the administrative effort required to make taxes that are tied to land ownership difficult to evade would appear to be comparatively small. The authorities need only to

[13] Some typical relief provisions of this type are noted above, pp. 52–53.

study the maps to determine whether each plot is on the tax rolls. In areas where field boundaries and titles are not clearly established and recorded, and where ground surveys are not immediately feasible, aerial photography usually affords a practical and speedy means of identifying ownership units and making rough estimates of their size. When government ownership records are inadequate, or when it is impossible to locate some owners, the tax assessment might be levied on the occupier or cultivator. Because of these opportunities for tax enforcement, identification of taxpayers and of taxable property need not be a serious barrier to effective collection of taxes imposed directly on the ownership or use of land, except in sections where there are no recognized rights in land or in sparsely populated regions characterized by nomadic agriculture. In the latter cases administrative considerations might favor a marketing tax or a capitation levy.

Second, the authorities will be aided in checking on taxpayer compliance if the form of the tax permits verification of the assessment on the basis of cadastral records or other official sources of information. Thus a tax that is assessed according to land value as established by official surveys, the results of which are made part of a permanent land record, would appear to be more easily enforced than one which relies upon field inspections at harvest time. In the latter case, verification of the assessment is difficult after the crop is gathered and marketed. The policing problem would seem to be even more troublesome for marketing taxes, since the object of assessment may escape detection and lose its identity after it moves into distribution channels. As noted above, some marketing taxes are dependent upon accurate record-keeping by registered traders, a requirement which has no counterpart under taxes assessed at the farm level.

Third, there is the problem of controlling delinquent taxpayers.[14] Many countries have had great difficulty in dealing with this problem, but the source of the difficulty seems to be largely

[14] Joseph P. Crockett has collected some revealing information on delinquencies in Paraguay; see p. 53, n. 16.

unrelated to the form of the tax. Because tax laws often fail to provide adequate penalties for nonpayment – or because tax officials are lax in applying these penalties – taxpayers often find that "the administrative machinery may bark, but that it has no bite." [15] As far as land taxes in general are concerned, they contain two features which are in themselves conducive to effective control over delinquencies: (1) the taxes are collected on a current basis, instead of on the basis of income or production in a prior year; and (2) land or its produce often stands as security for the tax and is subject to forfeiture to the government for taxes due.

Summary and Conclusions

It has been shown that the most formidable administrative problems of land taxation can be resolved in combination with the establishment of a satisfactory system of land administration. The soundest starting point for the taxation of land value or produce at the farm level is the cadastral survey and the accompanying register of land rights. Countries which tax land value without the benefit of adequate land maps and records of land use and ownership must rely upon market-value appraisals by local assessors or self-assessments by landowners; these countries have poor records of collection and enforcement. Where cadastral records are unsatisfactory, resort can also be had to tax assessments by field inspection at harvest time, but this method is costly and open to abuse. The remaining alternative of tax collection at the marketing stage instead of at the farm level might appeal to some countries on administrative grounds, although the record of experience with marketing taxes suggests that tax evasion and official corruption are difficult to control under such taxes.

Tax compliance is fostered by assessments that are based upon objective and easily verifiable criteria, as well as by enforcement

[15] Surrey, p. 19.

procedures which are effective in controlling delinquencies. But the two ingredients of successful administration which count for more than all the others are not provisions of the tax laws; they are, of course, the quality of the tax staff and the co-operativeness of the taxpaying community.

· PART THREE ·

PATHWAYS TO REFORM

X

BASIC DESIGN FOR MORE EFFECTIVE LAND TAXATION

A CRUEL IRONY of the development process is that the most pressing revenue needs arise in the early stages of a country's economic development when its taxable capacity is severely limited. For today's less developed countries, there is no escape from the fact that economic development, from its start, is a "greedy absorber of revenue." [1] In these countries an expanded tax-financed public sector is as necessary for a higher rate of capital formation as is the latter for economic growth. The governments must provide a substantial portion of the initial investment needs, especially "social overhead" projects, if they are to succeed in setting in motion a cumulative expansion process; at the same time, because of the generally low level of voluntary saving, much of the required saving for financing the investment must be forced by increased taxation as the best way to avoid having saving forced by a crippling inflation.[2]

The underdeveloped countries' search for additional revenue

[1] Ursula K. Hicks, "The Search for Revenue in Underdeveloped Countries," *Revue de Science et de Législation Financières* (1952). There is ample statistical support for the view that "wherever economic development has taken place the ratio of tax burden to national income has increased. . ." (Henry S. Bloch, "The Relation of Tax Policy to Economic Growth," in *The Limits of Taxable Capacity*, Tax Institute, Princeton, N. J., 1953, p. 171). Also see Henry G. Aubrey, "The Role of the State in Economic Development," *American Economic Review*, Papers and Proceedings (May 1951), pp. 266–273.

[2] See, for example, Ragnar Nurkse, *Problems of Capital Formation in Underdeveloped Countries* (Oxford, 1953), pp. 152–154.

has proceeded at an accelerated tempo since World War II. The results are apparent in the phenomenal revival of an old revenue source, export levies, and the gradual opening up of a new source, income and profits taxes. But another of the old favorites, land taxes, has lost substantial ground as a producer of revenue, while the remaining traditional source, sales and turnover taxes, seems largely to have held its own.

As explained in Chapter III, the general decline in the relative importance of land taxes in the fiscal systems of the underdeveloped countries can be attributed partly to the characteristic inflexibility and rate rigidity of most land taxes and partly to a deliberate policy of favoring new export and income taxes over increases in land taxes.[3] The latter policy, however, would seem to entail grave fiscal hazards for a country undertaking a major development program. In the first place, export taxes, while a flourishing revenue source in recent years when world demand for industrial raw materials and foods has been strong, are not a particularly dependable means of financing a permanently higher level of government expenditures. Export taxes are useful fiscal instruments in many ways, but as a source of development financing they should be backstopped by taxes with more assured yields. Second, although the underdeveloped countries should continue to work toward extending and strengthening their income taxes, they should also recognize that the establishment of a broadly based and effective income tax productive of large revenues will probably remain beyond the administrative competence of most of them for many years to come. Furthermore, income taxes with high marginal rates may run the risk of blunting investment incentives.

The aim of this final part of the study is to show that a properly conceived and applied land tax offers a promising solution to some pressing fiscal problems of underdeveloped countries. Though the most tangible result of more effective land taxation

[3] See above, p. 63.

would probably be the additional revenue yield and the elimination of tax deterrents to agricultural production, more equitable treatment of taxpayers and other salutary economic effects (such as encouraging the commercialization of agriculture) would also be important benefits. Furthermore, a strengthened land tax could provide desirable support for *local* government, which might brace the country's political health, and it could be an antidote to the temptation to collectivize agriculture in order to raise large revenue from the agricultural sector. For these important reasons, reform of existing land taxes deserves a high priority in government agenda almost everywhere.

The Place of Land Taxation in the Fiscal System

The amount of revenue needed to be raised is the logical starting point for tax legislation. In setting the revenue goal a basic consideration is the economic function of taxes in freeing productive resources from private use and making them available for government programs. As tax collections are stepped up, more resources tend to be released (except to the extent that the additional taxes are paid from funds that would otherwise have remained idle). Generally speaking, in countries seeking to accelerate their economic growth, the optimum revenue goal is exceedingly large relative to any realistic appraisal of the amount of revenue that can in fact be raised. These countries must therefore seek to tap practically every available revenue source; at the same time, of course, they must be constantly on guard against tax policies which, by discouraging or distorting production, would sap their economic strength. The higher the ratio of total revenue requirements to the national income, the more limited is the freedom of choice among different types of taxes, while every effect that taxes might produce grows in significance.

The very size of the agricultural sector in most countries creates a strong presumption that a substantial portion of the required revenue should be raised in that sector. Exactly how large that portion should be depends upon the level and distribution of agricultural income and upon agriculture's place in the over-all development plan. How large is the income surplus above basic living needs which might be absorbed through taxation? What rate of agricultural taxation would be most consistent with the expected transfer of resources from agriculture to industry as development occurs? What are the promising sources of growth in the agricultural sector, and how rapid a growth can be anticipated? Will agriculture reap special benefits from the development program and how fast will these benefits raise the practicable level of taxation in agriculture? The revenue potential of taxes on agriculture hinges on the answers to such basic questions as these.

Once the revenue goal for the agricultural sector is set, the government is ready to assess the means for meeting that goal. Specific questions of equity, economic effects, and administrative feasibility are important at this stage of tax policy-making. Although it is not possible to examine here each fiscal tool which might be employed to absorb funds from the agricultural sector, it may be useful to list the wide variety of available measures: (1) various types of land and produce taxes; (2) separate income taxes on agriculture or inclusion of agricultural income under a global income tax; (3) export taxes and multiple exchange rates affecting agriculture; (4) property transfer taxes; (5) general or selective sales taxes which burden the agriculturalist as consumer or producer; (6) mandatory deliveries of agricultural commodities to the government at low fixed prices; (7) fiscal monopolies, including government marketing boards; and (8) betterment levies, which might be imposed whenever the benefits of development projects are localized. To be sure, while most of the measures in this list have wide applicability, not all of them would be appropriate in all countries.

A prudent fiscal policy requires selecting the best possible combination of revenue measures rather than relying on any one measure alone. In its basic design the combination should probably provide for: (1) a means of mass taxation which would raise large amounts from a broad segment of the agricultural population without imposing excessive burdens on particular groups; (2) a more exclusive tax applying to the wealthier recipients of agricultural income; (3) one or more taxes designed to tap windfall incomes arising out of fluctuations in export prices or out of domestic developments; and (4) special taxes for regulatory purposes.

Assuming the existence of taxable capacity in the agricultural sector, what are the conditions which contribute to giving the land tax an important place in a country's plan for taxing that sector? The first basic condition relates to the tenure under which land is held and to the structure of agricultural production. Taxes based upon the ownership or use of land are difficult to administer in areas where land rights are not recorded, where no established rights in land are recognized, or where cultivation is done by nomadic tribes. Similarly, such taxes may not be feasible in sparsely settled areas which have not been adequately surveyed and where land is worked by squatters.

Second, it should be established that the circumstances within the country are not favorable for the collection of a fiscally productive personal income tax on farmers. Where favorable circumstances do exist – as, for example, in some plantation economies – preference should be given to the income tax, while the land tax might be used, if at all, as a subordinate levy set aside for local governments. Only a few countries, however, can raise large amounts of revenue with an income tax on agriculture. Farmers generally do not keep accounts, they often consume a good part of their output themselves, production expenses are difficult to verify, and there is no opportunity for collection at source – these are among the more obvious obstacles which generally prevent the income tax from becoming the main tool of agricultural tax policy in underdeveloped countries.

A third general condition likely to favor reliance upon land taxes is the presence of a large nonmonetary economy in agriculture. In addition to forming a barrier to broad-based income taxation, as noted above, this condition prevents the government from reaching the agricultural population through large-scale use of indirect taxes.

Fourth, an important place may be indicated for land taxes when the government is not disposed to undertake the actual collection and marketing of agricultural products. In several countries, notably Burma, Taiwan, and some countries in Africa, the governments obtain large revenues through carrying out these functions. Many governments, however, are unprepared to assume functions normally performed by private traders.

Finally, unless a country exports a significant portion of its agricultural output, export levies do not provide an effective alternative to land taxation. Where agricultural exports are large, however, a careful weighing of the respective advantages of each approach is called for. The choice between taxing exports and taxing land is not a matter of indifference, from the standpoint of either the government or the taxpayers, since the two approaches are not at all similar in their administrative requirements, economic effects, and distributional aspects. Even in export economies, the two approaches have more important complementary relationships than they do substitutional relationships with one another.

Generally speaking, the underdeveloped countries suffer from a poverty of acceptable alternatives as regards methods of taxing the agricultural sector. With relatively few exceptions, some form of land tax offers the only practicable and dependable means of obtaining the large amounts of revenue required from that sector. Moreover, in those fortunate countries actually having a choice among two or more methods of meeting their revenue goal for agricultural taxation, a decision favoring extensive reliance upon land taxes seems highly probable, even though other methods may also deserve a place.

Most governments are likely to attach considerable importance to the advantages of land taxes in these principal respects: (1)

their revenue potential is comparatively large because they can be applied broadly to all of agriculture; (2) being of versatile design, they are more readily adaptable than alternative taxes to serving a variety of equity and economic objectives; (3) they provide a means of breaking down the tax collection barriers of a large nonmonetary sector, illiteracy among the population, and low standards of living; (4) the liable taxpayers can usually be easily identified; and (5) the land (or its products) stands as security for the tax. Almost all countries, in addition, can draw upon previous experience with some sort of land tax to fashion a new land tax that can become an effective instrument of development financing. Even when the conditions within a country are singularly congenial to land taxation, however, there will still be a place for other forms of agricultural taxes as part of a balanced fiscal "package" for the agricultural sector.

Experience with land taxes teaches that it is invariably a laborious and painstaking task to build them into efficient and productive instruments of agricultural taxation. The three main problem areas in which satisfactory solutions have proved hardest to reach within the limits set by administrative and institutional factors are: (1) rationalization of the tax base, (2) adaptation to changes in prices and production, and (3) allowances for the personal and economic status of the individual taxpayer. The following sections outline ways in which the desired solutions may be found in different country settings. In the concluding chapter the opportunities for nonfiscal uses of land taxes in furtherance of specific agricultural and development goals will be described.

Rationalization of the Tax Base

For various reasons, the land tax has been relatively untouched by the twentieth-century trend toward taxes based upon income as best fitted to promote justice in taxation and maximum economic growth. "In land revenue policy," writes a student of Indian taxation, "habit and precedent have accounted for more than wisdom."[4] In addition to short-sighted expediency and administrative inertia, certain conceptual fallacies have militated against the application of modern principles of taxation to land taxes. These fallacies are epitomized in the *in rem* doctrine which holds that "personalizing" the land tax would corrupt its essential character as a tax on a "gift of nature" and on a source of "unearned increment." Time and again this doctrine has been mistakenly used to justify a special status for land taxes in the family of revenue instruments. Before important headway can be made with land tax reform, this type of thinking must be discarded in favor of the view that the same basic criteria of equitableness are applicable to land taxes as to other taxes.

Although many of the trappings of modern income taxation – such as self-assessment on the basis of the taxpayer's records of income and expenses – cannot be generally applied in taxing agricultural income in the less developed countries, certain basic income tax principles can be adhered to.[5] The all-important concept of a tax related to individual taxpaying capacity need not be sacrificed in its entirety, though precise measurement of the tax base must of course yield to measurement within the limits of administrative feasibility in each country.

The most valuable and efficient tool for a successful reconstruction of land taxation, giving particular emphasis to rationalizing the tax base, is a system of soil classification and rating according to indices of productive capacity and relative income potential. A country able to carry out that basic step – or else to adopt other land classification methods which, though less satisfactory than the more advanced techniques, will still give reasonable recognition to differences in the productive capacity of

[4] B. Das Gupta, *Provincial Taxation under Autonomy* (Calcutta, 1945), p. 298.

[5] See Walter W. Heller, "The Adaptation of Income Taxation to Agriculture in Underdeveloped Countries," *Papers and Proceedings of the Conference on Agricultural Taxation and Economic Development* (Cambridge, 1954), pp. 270–282.

land – can then apply an appropriate taxing formula and, if desired, introduce adjustments for personal exemptions and allowances. Further modifications to soften the tax impact on new productive investment can also be allowed.[6]

The following suggestions for reform of the tax base are not relevant to a tax on agricultural marketings, as imposed in some Middle Eastern countries in lieu of direct taxes on land. While a marketing tax may represent the only feasible means of collecting large revenues from agriculture in countries where farming regions have not been surveyed and where there are no established ownership and tenure rights in land, such a tax is an essentially primitive and potentially harsh type of levy. Although a marketing tax includes a built-in exemption of the farmer's own consumption, it offers none of the opportunities for direct application of income tax principles. Moreover, a marketing tax tends to discourage the movement of produce to the cities and may be damaging to agricultural output because of its effects on marginal producers.

The first step in the administration of direct taxes on land is the identification of taxable fields and taxpayers. This subject has already been treated in earlier chapters.[7] Some countries do not have satisfactory land maps and their records of land ownership and field boundaries are inaccurate and incomplete. Such conditions not only impede reform of land taxation but also stand as a barrier to improvement of many important phases of land administration (e.g., controlling tenancy conditions, surveying land use, planning agrarian reforms) and to the development of a system of land-based credit. Land mapping and the preparation of property registers would seem to deserve a top priority, therefore, whenever major land tax improvements or other agricultural assistance programs are contemplated.

[6] Although some of these modifications would entail revisions of the tax base, they are not treated in this section but are reserved for discussion as "nonfiscal applications" in Chapter XI.

[7] See especially Chapter IX, pp. 165, 172–173.

Soil Classification According to Productive Capacity[8]

Classifying soil according to its productive capacity is largely without precedent in those countries, mostly in Latin America, which employ property taxes based presumably on the selling price of land. Productivity classifications are a familiar practice, however, in many Asian and European countries. The present proposal involves a change in the mode of expression of the tax base in countries having such classifications, but not necessarily any fundamental changes in their present land survey techniques. Instead of gross produce, net produce, or rental value, what is proposed here is a yardstick based upon potential net income.

The following description starts with an outline of the basic approach as it might be applied in a country which would not encounter any obstacles because of the expense and technical skills required for its implementation. Admittedly, few of the poorer countries are in so fortunate a position as to be free of such obstacles. The ideal plan must therefore be viewed as a goal which may be far off for the least developed countries but already within the reach of some that are fairly well advanced. The discussion later turns to possible auxiliary standards and compromising methods which would carry out at least some features of the basic proposal.

The present plan calls for two types of soil classifications: (1) in terms of inherent soil characteristics and (2) in terms of economic use capabilities.[9] The first type entails scientific soil

[8] For samples of recent manuals on classification of agricultural land for tax purposes the reader is referred to: *A Procedure for the Equitable Assessment of Nebraska Farm Land,* Quentin W. Lindsey, Agricultural Experiment Station, University of Nebraska, Lincoln, Nebraska (Bulletin 400, December 1950) and *Procedure for Land Reclassification in Montana,* Montana State College Agricultural Experiment Station, Bozeman, Montana (Bulletin 459, February 1949). The German system of land classification, which is also followed to a considerable extent in Finland, is similar to that described in this section. See N. Westermarck, "Economic Problems in the Classification of Land," *Proceedings of the Eighth International Conference of Agricultural Economists* (Oxford University Press, 1953), pp. 253–264, and subsequent discussion, pp. 265–269.

[9] See *Land Classification for Agricultural Development,* Development

mapping to determine the entire sequence of soil layers, from the surface down, known as the "soil profile." Soil mapping is most important, of course, in the case of crop land, but it can also show whether pastures, timberland, orchards, brushland, and so on, are suitable for particular crops. Soil is generally distinguishable by strata often markedly different in such obvious characteristics as texture (sand, silt, clay, etc.), structure (loose, granular, compact), and color (red, yellow, gray, black, etc.). Among the physical, chemical, and biological characteristics which are ordinarily considered to be of outstanding importance in crop production are the following: depth of entire profile, texture, permeability, thickness of top soil, moisture-holding capacity, degrees of acidity or alkalinity, natural drainage, natural plant-nutrient content, organic matter content, degree of erosion, and salinity.[10] Because of the relative permanency of these natural characteristics, soil mapping, if done properly, will ordinarily be valid for many years ahead. Occasional updating will be necessary, however, to allow for changes in the drainage situation, sedimentation, erosion, and land improvement programs, and for basic shifts in land use which may attach importance to soil properties not previously considered significant.

The use-capability classification, which is the second type, builds upon the scientific soil classification. Its purpose is to group soil types according to their capacity for producing various crops. It should allow not only for such factors as relationship to potential water supply, climate, position of land with respect to sunshine and shadow, topography, and size, shape, and slope of fields, but also for the types of agriculture practiced in the area, the skills possessed by the farmers living there, and the availability of various farm implements. The entire farm should be considered as a unit for the determination of the most feasible use of the land.

Paper No. 18, Food and Agriculture Organization of the United Nations (November 1952).

[10] *Ibid.*, pp. 15–16.

Ratings According to Presumptive Net Income

After the most feasible land use for each delineated area of each tract has been determined, the area should be assigned a rating in accordance with its potential net income under average growing conditions and proper management.[11] At this step allowances should be introduced for necessary crop rotation and for market factors (distance from markets, existence of access roads, and availability of storage and milling facilities). The potential output of each soil type must be valued in terms of an assumed selling price, and input costs (exclusive of the value of the labor of the farmer and his family) must be estimated in detail and expressed in monetary equivalents. Realistic quantitative valuations are unnecessary, however; instead, the ratings might be based upon index numbers, since the ultimate objective of an equitable allocation of the tax load will be served if the income potential of the given land area is represented simply as a ratio to the income potential of a standard producing unit (which should ordinarily be the top producing soil for each recognized use). It is important, of course, to have the original soil and use-capability classifications in the proper form so that the necessary net income relationships can be calculated.

The use of yardstick farms, as found in parts of Central Europe, can be a valuable aid at various stages of the rating process. The operating results on these farms can be used for verifying yield potentials and input requirements on different soil types. If the farms are operated as agricultural experiment stations, they can also serve valuable scientific purposes, such as the development of improved seeds and better techniques of cultivation.

Multiplying the land area in each taxable tract by the assigned rating will provide an index of the income potential of the tract.

[11] The use of potential instead of actual net income, while not strictly in accord with ability-to-pay principles, seems necessary on practical grounds, and it might also be advocated because of its desirable incentive effects. Farmers deriving less than the full potential would be penalized by the tax, while those exceeding the rated potential would not be taxed on the excess.

A tax rate formula can then be applied to determine the basic tax assessment. As the final step, adjustments might be made for additional factors entering into the determination of each individual's tax liability (see below).[12]

In order to protect the taxpayers against unfair and inequitable assessments, review committees, composed of local farmers appointed by the district tax collectors, might be established in each jurisdiction. Several countries employ committees of this type, to serve as boards of appeal and also to advise the taxing authorities on local conditions. Local committees can also aid in the administration of relief provision for hardship situations created by drought, insect damage, and other catastrophes.

Substitute Procedures

It would be unrealistic to suggest that the above proposal for scientific soil classification and economic rating is a thoroughly practical plan for most of today's underdeveloped countries.[13] The requirements for its early and successful implementation in all of its phases are doubtless prohibitive for many of these countries – perhaps even for most of them. The plan is presented as a target on which the underdeveloped countries – and many developed ones, too – should set their sights, provided the preconditions for heavy reliance upon land taxation are present.[14] Without question, the plan is impossible of swift adoption in countries which have had no previous experience with cadastral surveys. Many countries may be stopped from putting it into effect because it would involve a larger investment of manpower and money than they are presently prepared to make, or because they would not be able to recruit a staff with the necessary tech-

[12] The basic approach outlined above is similar to that explained in A. R. Aandahl, W. G. Murray, and W. Scholtes, "Economic Rating of Soils for Tax Assessment," *Journal of Farm Economics* (August 1954), pp. 483–499.

[13] It should be noted that the plan would need to be modified where bush and tree crops are involved, because of the long waiting time between investment and the realization of income.

[14] See above, pp. 183–184.

nical skills. Still, it would be to their advantage to agree upon a target plan of land taxation and to move toward it as rapidly as they can. It is appropriate, therefore, to review various substitute procedures which, by building upon the existing land tax systems wherever possible, would be in general keeping with the approach just outlined and would result in substantial improvements in the existing systems. The substitutes described below are more than expedients, however; they are designed to serve as stepping-stones toward the ideal plan.

Ratings Based upon Gross Produce. One possibility which has attractions for some countries is to tie the land tax assessment to gross produce. Because of its simplicity gross output is widely used as a valuation basis for many purposes. In various sections of India, Pakistan, and Burma, for example, rents are customarily based upon gross output in kind, and countries which have mandatory marketings of farm produce often set quotas according to estimates of the gross output of each field. Thus, there is considerable experience with that type of measurement. Either the actual harvest or some standard or "normal" yield might serve, although administrative and incentive considerations would seem to favor the latter. Taxation of the annual harvest instead of a calculated "normal" yield comes nearer to direct assessment of each farmer's net income, but "it compels the tax administration to exert wider supervision than . . . presumptive systems." [15]

Land classification records, preferably based upon cadastral maps and field surveys of land productivity, might provide the necessary data for rating each field according to its "normal" yield; alternatively, resort might be had to official records of the average harvest of each field in a base period, provided the records are reasonably accurate. In addition, a crude land classification system used in conjunction with unit yield tables (i.e., schedules showing expected gross output per unit of land area in each classification) might work fairly well in many

[15] League of Nations, Fiscal Committee, *Technical Principles of Taxation: Income Tax Practice* (Report of June 15, 1940), p. 42.

countries; the yield potential could be calculated by multiplying the area of the field by the indicated unit yield of land of a given grade in a given location with respect to rainfall and temperature.

An instructive illustration of how the latter method might be applied is provided by a proposed land tax law to replace the marketing tax in Iraq.[16] Although sections of Iraq have not yet been surveyed and the land settlement records are incomplete and often out-of-date, the Ministry of Finance was able to formulate, with the aid of technical assistance advisers, a land tax plan that was considered workable and requires assessments according to indicated average yield. The proposed tax (*Kharaj*) is at the rate of 10 per cent of the average yield per donum of land. Land would be classified as follows:

Class 1. *Rain Lands*: Lands which are usually cropped with complete reliance on rain. These lands are divided into four grades, according to the altitude above sea level and the average rainfall. Each grade is subdivided into "very fertile," "of medium fertility," and "of poor fertility."

Class 2. *Flow Rain Lands*: Lands which receive an average rainfall of less than 200 millimeters yearly and which get, without lifts, flow waters which enable them to be cultivated with summer crops. These lands are divided into two grades, depending upon the continuity of the flow waters, and each grade is subdivided into three fertility classes, as above.

Class 3. *Flow Lands*: Lands (excluding rice lands) which receive a minimum rainfall and are irrigated by regular and irregular flow waters, including tidal waters. These lands are divided into three grades, according to when the canals are opened and the regularity of the flow, and are subdivided into three fertility classes.

Class 4. *Lands Irrigated by Lift*: Lands (excluding rice lands)

[16] "Draft of Land Tax Law for Iraq," International Program in Taxation, Harvard Law School (October 1957), mimeographed. This document was furnished by the United States Operations Mission in Baghdad in 1956. As of the end of 1957, the law had not been enacted.

irrigated by different types of lifts, or by horse power, from rivers, wells, and other water sources. These lands are divided into three grades, according to the efficiency of the irrigation systems, and are subdivided into three fertility classes.

Class 5. *Rice Lands*: Lands which are inundated with flood waters and are fit for rice cultivation year after year. These lands are divided into four grades, according to the adequacy of the water supply, and are subdivided into three fertility classes.

Class 6. *Gardens*: Lands containing a minimum of 20 fruit-bearing date palms or trees. These lands are divided into five grades according to the number and kinds of trees, and each grade is subdivided into four classes also depending upon the number and kinds of trees. There is a fifth grade which covers vineyards and is subdivided by type of irrigation and kinds of vines.

Class 7. *Pastures*: These are divided into three grades according to the quality of the pasture land.

Class 8. *Forests*: These are divided into three grades and additional subgrades according to the density of the forests.

Class 9. *Uncultivated Lands*: Lands which are fit for cultivation but are not cultivated. These lands are divided into two grades and additional subgrades according to the average rainfall, availability of irrigation, and density of the trees on the land.

Class 10. *Lands Not Fit for Cultivation*: These are rocky, desert, sandy, or saline lands, or marshes; also, they include other lands which, because of location, are not suitable for cultivation.

The above system of classification provides a total of ninety separate classes of land. However, the administrative task would not be as complex as this large total might suggest, since the number of classes in any one region would be much smaller than in the country as a whole.

The proposed law specifies the actual amount of tax due per donum on each class and grade of land, in terms of staple crops (wheat, barley, and rice), dates, grapes, or firewood. The Minister of Finance would be given the option of collecting the tax in kind or in cash, and if it is to be the latter, he would announce the prices to be used in converting the assessment into monetary terms.

An interesting feature of this draft law is that the taxpayers will be required to submit statements showing the areas and classes of their lands. These statements will be received by classification committees who will inspect the lands and study other available information bearing on the potential yield before certifying the classifications to the Minister of Finance. The law provides that the classification and the tax that is charged would generally remain unchanged for five years.

One method of making taxes of the type described above, as well as others that are assessed on an average yield basis, more closely consistent with the principle of rating according to presumptive net income would be to determine each farmer's tax not on the basis of estimated *gross* produce of his field, but rather on the basis of a *fraction* of that amount. The fraction that is used should vary for fields in different classifications and locations, in order to allow for indicated inequalities in income earning potential (after production costs). This added refinement should not encounter any large administrative obstacles, and it would substantially strengthen the equitableness of the tax.[17]

Ratings Derived from Annual Rental Value. In those countries having land taxes that are assessed according to annual rental value as established by scientific land classification surveys, it may not be a major undertaking to convert the tax base to the new standard here proposed. In some parts of India and Pakistan, for example, much of the raw information needed for rating the fields on a relative net income basis may already exist. The principal disadvantage of a well-administered rental value approach, in addition to its mistaken conceptual origin, is that it applies, at least in theory, only to land rent and therefore ignores earned

[17] A plan of land taxation based upon varying proportions of normal gross produce was proposed for Burma by Sir Bernard Ottwell Binns, *Agricultural Economy in Burma* (Rangoon, 1948), pp. 45–48.

income. Thus, the tax base is too narrow and not in accord with ability-to-pay.

It would probably not be feasible, on the other hand, to derive the proposed new ratings directly from the revenue "settlement" which is likely to be long outdated. In considering the pattern of land revenue settlements in India, for example, the recent Taxation Enquiry Commission stressed that the pattern in such states as Madras and Bombay is based in part "on the chronological accident as to when each [area] was settled or resettled." [18] In its recommendations for land revenue reform, therefore, the Commission placed heavy stress upon a scheme for standardizing the different assessment levels by increasing the existing assessment according to a formula based upon the change in the price level since the last settlement or resettlement was made.[19]

Furthermore, a rental value tax base that simply reflects past, or even current, market rents and is not backstopped by cadastral information on the factors determining the productive capacity of the land cannot readily be converted to the new system until the necessary cadastral surveys are made. Because of the variety of prevailing rental arrangements and the notorious imperfections of the rental markets for agricultural land in almost all countries, rental values that are not supported at least by rudimentary soil surveys and land-use capability classifications are not satisfactory guides for rating land for tax purposes.[20]

Net rental value, calculated on the basis of actual rental receipts less a reasonable estimate of the landlord's out-of-pocket expenses for management, measures presumptive net rental income and is therefore an appropriate tax base for landlords having only rental income, but not for landlords having both rental and other income, or for farmers who are owner-operators. In countries where much of the agricultural land is controlled by large land-

[18] *Report of the Taxation Enquiry Commission, 1953–54* (Government of India, 1955), III, 210.

[19] *Ibid.*, 226–227.

[20] See above, pp. 15–17.

lords, it would seem feasible to include either presumptive or actual net rental income under a general income tax and to scale down the land tax accordingly.

Ratings Derived from Sales Value of Land. It is extremely difficult to construct an equitable and efficient system of land taxation by relying primarily on information on the selling price of land. There are relatively few sales in any single year in comparison with the number of fields to be appraised, and the selling prices very often do not reflect true market valuations.[21] A genuinely competitive land market, with active trading among buyers and sellers, exists in only a relatively few countries.

Sales values, carefully sorted for their reliability as evidence of market values, may be a useful source of information, but they are no satisfactory substitute for valuations based upon the soil profile, topography, size, shape, location, and economic characteristics of each holding. In recent years several sections of the United States have undertaken land classification surveys for property tax assessment.[22] The many countries in Latin America and elsewhere which employ capital value assessments should initiate a similar reform in order to put their property taxes on a sound footing and to make them more effective revenue producers. The necessary land surveys should be made and the physical data for each field converted into a realistic estimate of market value. Once that step is completed it would not be difficult to go further and establish economic ratings in terms of potential net income.

Area Taxes with Classified Rates. A simplified approach, which may appeal to countries unable to undertake scientific soil

[21] A recent study of the land market in India, H. C. Mukerji, "A Study of the Variation of Land Prices in South Calcutta," *Journal of the Institution of Engineers* (India), October 1956, pp. 57–70, underlines the scarcity of reliable land market data in urban areas, not to mention farming areas, in underdeveloped countries.

[22] See William G. Murray, "New Developments in Farm Appraisal for Loans and Tax Assessments," *Journal of Farm Economics*, Proceedings Issue (November 1951), pp. 857–865.

mapping and economic rating of land, is to classify each field on the basis of its potential use and by easily recognizable criteria bearing upon its fertility and ease of cultivation, and to graduate the tax rate according to the land classification. Relatively few classifications may suffice in comparatively homogeneous agricultural regions, but a large number may be needed to achieve equitable results in areas marked by wide differences in soil types, climate, rainfall, and kinds of products. In West Jordan, for example, agricultural land is divided into sixteen categories, but in Ethiopia only four categories are recognized.[23] Even sixteen classes, however, would seem to be a relatively small number in most countries if adequate recognition is given to important differences in land value.

The tax should be stated as an amount per unit of area in each standard classification.[24] The tax rate schedule should be designed so that the differentials among the classes correspond as closely as possible with the relative income potential of each class of land. At best, only a rough correspondence is possible, yet this method may prove to be the only feasible means of introducing at least a modicum of equity in the distribution of the land tax burden in some countries today. Moreover, the system of graduated rates should be conducive to more efficient land use. The method would assure substantially better results than are possible with the loosely administered property taxes in many countries, and it deserves serious consideration there as a less expensive alternative to scientific soil surveys and use-capability classifications.

The adoption of simplified land taxes which differentiate among broad categories of land use may soon be given a boost by the growing use of aerial photography in preparing a reason-

[23] See Chapter I, pp. 12–13.

[24] Although the draft land tax law for Iraq, discussed on pages 193–195, fixes an amount of tax per unit of area in each classification, the basic provision that imposes tax does so in terms of a percentage of average yield. It is apparent that those who drafted the law thought that a refined classified rate area tax was the practical equivalent of a tax based on average yield.

ably satisfactory and inexpensive land classification. Besides, aerial photography can be used to determine approximate field boundaries in areas which have not been surveyed. It is also of proven value in speeding actual soil survey work, which involves identifying soil boundaries which are then checked in the field, although it requires judicious use and expert interpretation.[25]

Tax Treatment of Landlords and Tenants

The preferred land tenure setting for a system of taxation based on land ratings according to potential net income is one in which the typical farmer is an owner-cultivator. These ratings do not offer so satisfactory a solution of the equity issue in countries where tenant farming is practiced, since the income potential of a rented field is shared by the landlord and tenant.

Farm tenancy has been declining in recent years, as a result of the redistributive effects of land reform, but it is still the dominant tenure form in a number of countries. How to achieve an appropriate distribution of the land tax between landlords and tenants is a problem with no easy answer in these countries, regardless of the type of land tax imposed. Distributions on the basis of individual allocations of the tax assessment between each landlord and his tenants are ordinarily out of the question for administrative reasons.

If the landlords are taxed according to the income potential of their holdings, it may not be intended that they should carry the full tax burden. It might be argued, on the one hand, that the landlord should be viewed as a tax withholding agent, in which case rental adjustments to shift some of the tax onto his tenants would be sanctioned. If the rental terms are subject to government control, as they are in many countries, the government has a convenient tool for regulating the extent of tax shifting from landlords to tenants. On the other hand, the government might

[25] See P. Buringh, "The Analysis of Pedological Elements in Aerial Photographs," *Transactions, Fifth International Congress of Soil Science* (Brussels, International Congress of Soil Science, 1954), vol. IV, pp. 90–91.

reject the withholding argument and use its powers to prevent shifting, on the ground that the landlords possess sufficient taxable capacity to carry the full tax without being unduly burdened. If there are no controls, the shifting would be determined by the interplay of economic and institutional forces. With tax shifting, however, there would be a danger of losing the chief advantage of the net income approach; the final resting place of the tax, after the shifting has worked itself out, need not correspond at all to the distribution of net income among landlords and their tenants.

It should be apparent that a policy of allocating the tax between landlords and tenants according to the proportion of the harvest paid as rent — assuming that rents are stated as a proportion of the harvest — would not prove satisfactory, simply because that proportion is unlikely to coincide with the allocation of production costs.

The arrangement which offers the best solution is to assess the tax against both land-owning groups and tenants having income above a minimum exemption level. The former would pay the full tax, but tenant-cultivators would be allowed a tax credit in recognition of their rental obligations. The tax credit should probably be standardized in order to avoid individual adjustments for each tenant according to his particular rental agreement. Landlords and owner-cultivators might be taxed on the same basis, even though the landlords do not cultivate all the land themselves. On the other hand, landlords might be given the option of paying instead an income tax on their rental income, provided they maintain adequate income and expense records.[26]

Assessing a land tax against a tenant is more difficult than assessing one against a landlord. For example, an unpaid land tax bill becomes a lien against the land. No enforcement measure

[26] Some writers favor an extra heavy tax on landlords because it would not endanger incentives and the absorption of landlords' savings would not curtail productive investment; for example, see W. Arthur Lewis, *The Theory of Economic Growth* (Homewood, Illinois, 1955), p. 400.

of this kind is available against a tenant. As here proposed, the land tax on a tenant would be in effect a personal tax on his presumptive net income. There are probably no grounds for taxing peasants in overpopulated countries where rental rates are high and tenant incomes so small as to fall below a reasonable minimum exemption level for the tax. Elsewhere, tenant incomes may contain a measure of taxable capacity which can be tapped more easily under a land tax than under a general income tax (or through indirect taxes). As for owners of large estates, a general income tax clearly is the more appropriate method of reaching them, except that they might still be assessed for a share of the land tax that is reserved for local government. Landowners who do not lease land on a large scale are in an in-between situation, and giving them an option as to the basis of taxation, as suggested above, would seem to be an appropriate solution.

Tax Adjustments for Hired Labor

A less important but somewhat analogous problem to that of the tax treatment of landlords and tenants arises on farms that are cultivated by hired labor. Like tenants, hired labor participates in the income that is produced on the land; therefore, it would not be logically correct to allocate the full presumptive income from a field to the employer-owner. One may be inclined to dismiss this problem by arguing that the employer will not necessarily bear the full tax because, if it is a heavy burden, he probably will be able to shift part of it to his workers through adjustments in wage rates. As in the case of shifting to tenants, the possibility exists for the government to impose wage controls which would restrict the shifting, but effective wage controls would seem to be more difficult than rent controls to administer. If there is tax shifting, the government may find it necessary to take positive steps to protect the welfare of agricultural laborers.

To allow tax credits for hired labor, similar to the credits suggested above for rental payments, would not be a workable arrangement if the labor is composed mostly of part-time and seasonal workers, since it would be virtually impossible to verify the claims for tax credits.

For the most part hired labor is a major cost item only on the larger and more profitable farms, or on farms with absentee owners. The impairment of equity because of the failure to adjust for labor costs may not be serious in these cases, since the owners of larger farms probably possess adequate taxable capacity to carry the full tax. As for the case of absentee owners, it is often argued that a tax penalty on absentee ownership is warranted on the ground that such ownership is detrimental to agricultural production. For these separate reasons, it would seem inadvisable to provide a special credit for hired labor; instead, the government should work to create a situation in which the larger farms can be included under an income tax and taxed on the basis of ascertained income with full allowance for actual production costs. Under the latter plan the income tax rates might be set to produce a higher tax liability than if the larger producing units had remained subject to the land tax. In a country where much of agriculture is organized on a plantation basis, the administrative arguments against income taxation of plantation owners may fade away on close scrutiny.[27]

Revenue Flexibility

Rationalization of the tax base, including improvement of the basic tools of assessment, is the most urgently needed type of land tax reform today. Without doubt the reform next in order of priority in most countries is to make the tax yield more responsive to price and production changes. Increased responsiveness will ordinarily increase the equitableness of the tax, but its main advantage lies in its economic effects. A flexible tax contributes to the goal of economic stability and it also serves the important function of diverting part of the increase in income, as a country's

[27] The experience in Travancore-Cochin, India, is a case in point; see *Report of the Taxation Enquiry Commission, 1953–54,* III, 197, 208.

development program bears fruit, to the financing of new development projects.

The inelasticity which characterizes most land taxes is organic; that is to say, it comes from within the tax, as a result of the application of a stable tax rate to a tax base that is not kept current. The inelasticity has never been ironclad, however, because of necessary tax remission in the event of agricultural disasters and crop failure through no fault of the cultivator, and because of variations in the efficiency of tax collection.

In the past, stability of yield has usually been considered a tax advantage for administrative reasons and because of the desire to have an assured source of revenue.[28] The event which did most to expose the disadvantages of revenue inflexibility was World War II and the postwar inflation; the resultant depreciation of land tax revenues is the root of many underdeveloped countries' financial difficulties in recent years. The expectation of an accelerated tempo of agricultural development, together with the appearance of new fiscal theories, has also contributed to the changed attitude toward flexibility.

Countries which employ a capital value base show little progress toward making land tax revenues more flexible. The practice in the American states of setting the property tax rate each year in accordance with budget requirements is not followed in many countries, probably because of inadequacies in the administrative machinery for their land taxes. Progress has been achieved, however, in several countries with land taxes based upon a rental value or production concept. The re-establishment of in-kind taxes in South Korea and Taiwan is, in part, a response to the fiscal havoc created by inflation; the yield of in-kind taxes automatically adjusts to price changes. On the Indo-Pakistan subcontinent, "sliding-scale systems" were introduced in Punjab

[28] Yield stability may still be an advantage when the tax is used for local expenditures on roads, education, and other essential services; however, the increase in the potential tax base as agricultural production expands should not be allowed to go untapped.

in 1935 and Sind in 1938; these systems, however, were brought on not by inflation but by the sharp price decline during the depression in the thirties. The method recently followed by some of the Indian states (Hyderabad, Punjab, and Madras) in order to siphon off part of the increase in agricultural income resulting from high prices has been to impose interim surcharges on the land revenues.[29]

It is easier to adjust the tax assessment for long-term price and production changes than for annual changes. Thus, the recent proposal of the Indian Taxation Enquiry Commission contemplates a revision of the land revenue assessment (after standardization) once every ten years with reference to changes in the price level. The proposed method of revision is intended to be "carried out more or less automatically on the basis of the price levels without the intervention of an elaborate administrative machinery operating on small units over long periods at disproportionate cost." [30] The Commission suggests a scale of land revenue adjustments in accordance with the change in the price of the predominant crop in the given region. Price changes of less than 25 per cent would be ignored; for larger changes the proposed revenue adjustments are proportionately bigger in the event of price declines than of price increases.

A scheme of this sort would seem to be within the competence of most underdeveloped countries imposing land taxes. However, it is only a partial solution for the problem of inflexibility, since it does not provide regular tax adjustments for changes in the level of production or for short-run fluctuations in price. What is really needed is a plan for annual revisions by means of an easily applied formula.[31] As a prerequisite, the standard assessments

[29] See *Report of the Taxation Enquiry Commission, 1953–54,* III, 197.
[30] *Ibid.,* p. 228.
[31] Perhaps the simplest type of adjustment is that recommended by the United Nations Technical Assistance Mission to Bolivia in 1951. The Mission proposed annual adjustments of assessed property values on the basis of an index of current property values prepared by the Ministry of Finance. The United Nations Economic Mission to Chile (1949–50) proposed an annual

should be free of gross inequities. If the land tax is assessed on the basis of relative net income, as proposed above, the formula could be applied either to the assessed value (which would have no meaning in itself except as an index of value) or to the amount of the tax for each field. The design of the formula should provide a scale of adjustments as production and prices change; a formula that was tied to production and not to prices, or to prices and not to production, would not be satisfactory because, at least in the short run, these variables tend to move inversely (e.g., a generally poor harvest will ordinarily bring high prices).

Precise adjustments would obviously be impracticable. It would suffice to be guided by broad price and production indexes which measure average changes, rather than to employ a series of individual commodity indexes. However, separate indexes might be computed for the principal agricultural regions in the country, not only to allow for climatic differences, but also to catch the differential impact of economic development on the various regions. Indexes of this type are likely to have independent usefulness for agricultural development planning. Small changes in the relevant indexes could be ignored, thus avoiding too frequent revisions of the tax.

"Personalizing" the Tax

Some countries can go much further than others in remaking their land taxes in the image of income taxes. If a country is not equipped to do any more than to impose a crudely assessed tax on capital value, it would seem incongruous for that country to attempt to "personalize" the tax by introducing allowances for the taxpayer's marital and dependency status and for other personal

adjustment of real estate values on the basis of either the average increase in the newly assessed values or of an index of sales values of real estate. The Chilean law requires cadastral assessments every 5 to 10 years. See summaries of technical assistance reports in *Taxes and Fiscal Policy in Underdeveloped Countries*, United Nations Technical Assistance Administration (New York, 1954), pp. 47–48, 55–56.

circumstances that bear upon his taxpaying capacity. On the other hand, a country that employs scientific land classification surveys and makes detailed corrections for economic factors need not stop at that point, but can go one step further and introduce adjustments for the taxpayers' personal circumstances. Such adjustments would expunge once and for all the *in rem* characteristics of the land tax.

As explained in earlier chapters, administrative, economic, and equity considerations argue for a minimum deduction as a tax-free allowance. The minimum deduction might be applied in different ways: (1) as a standard deduction against the taxable value of each field; (2) as a standard deduction for each taxpayer, so that a person owning more than a single field would still be entitled to only one deduction; (3) as a per capita deduction, so that each taxpayer would receive a total deduction corresponding to the number of persons living off the fields which he works;[32] and (4) as a deduction varying according to the number of a taxpayer's dependents but not necessarily on a per capita basis. A similar set of possibilities exist under the alternative approach of providing tax credits instead of deductions from the tax base.

The administrative burdens of a plan for personal deductions or credits should not be underestimated. The taxpayer's marital and dependency status is subject to frequent changes and in countries where marriages, births, and deaths are not always recorded, the problem of preventing abuse may be troublesome. It would probably be advisable to make each taxpayer responsible for reporting changes in his own status. In addition, a possible simplification would be to establish a few dependency classes (e.g., one to two persons, three to five persons, and six or more persons) rather than to vary the deduction with the actual

[32] Per capita deductions, expressed in terms of quantities of grain, are provided in sections of Mainland China, where progressive tax rates are also in force. See Joseph N. Froomkin, "Structure and Taxation of Agriculture in China," *Conference on Agricultural Taxation*, p. 420.

number in the family. An important feature of an equitable plan – to bring together all land parcels belonging to each individual, so that his tax assessments may be aggregated and there is no incentive to splitting up holdings – is rarely observed anywhere.

An instance of recognition of the taxpayer's personal circumstances is found in some countries which have just completed a land reform. In South Korea, for example, where new landowners paid for their land in five annual installments, each amounting to 30 per cent of the annual harvest, a five-point reduction from the standard tax schedule was allowed.[33]

Some countries may wish to consider allowances for other factors affecting the individual's taxpaying capacity, such as interest on loans and losses due to fire and other catastrophes. Such allowances should of course be restricted to factors having a genuine and appreciable effect upon capacity.

The heavier the tax, the more compelling is the need for personal allowances; on the other hand, failure of the tax law to recognize valid differences among taxpayers will limit the tax to a lower yield than is necessary. It would be mistaken, therefore, to assume that provision of allowances will always involve a sacrifice of revenue; instead, it may pave the way for a broadening of the tax base and for rate increases.

Summary and Conclusions

This chapter has proposed an overhauling of the land tax in line with modern principles of taxation and fiscal policy as interpreted in the setting of underdeveloped economies. The goal sought is a tax that recognizes, within the limits of a country's administrative capabilities, individual differences in ability-to-pay,

[33] Haskell P. Wald, "The Recent Experience of the Republic of Korea with Tax Collections in Kind," *Conference on Agricultural Taxation*, p. 428. In many other countries, however, no concessions were made to ease the transitional effects of land reforms. See Philip M. Raup, "Agricultural Taxation and Land Reform in Underdeveloped Countries," *ibid.*, p. 265.

and that also serves, in combination with other taxes on agriculture, as an efficient instrument for mobilizing savings for capital formation. The more closely the tax measures up to that goal, the greater the likelihood of its attracting taxpayer cooperation in its administration and the easier it will be for the government to build the tax into an effective revenue producer.

Three sets of recommendations have been made, to be pursued at as fast a pace as local circumstances permit: first, to reform the tax base and to improve the methods of assessment, so that the tax rests on a sound land classification system and accords as closely as possible with presumptive net income; second, to make the tax yield responsive to changes in prices and production; and third, to relate the tax liability, to the extent practicable, to the personal circumstances of the taxpayer. These recommendations take for granted that countries with weak administrative organizations and defective land records will take corrective steps in these vital areas before moving ahead with the more progressive reforms.

The design of the recommendations envisages continuous progress toward bringing much of agricultural income under a country-wide income tax. Starting with the corporate enterprises, where they exist in agriculture, and then with the managers of plantations and the wealthier landlords (at least with respect to their rental and interest income), a country should seek gradually to supplement the land tax with an income tax based on ascertained net income and supported by the necessary taxpayers' accounting records. The combined yield from the income and land taxes should grow in the process, partly because of the expected expansion of agricultural production and the continuous improvement of tax collection methods. With the extended coverage of the income tax, the land tax will tend to recede in importance. It may eventually apply primarily to agriculturalists earning more than a bare subsistence but not enough to warrant direct assessment of income by the taxing authorities, or it may be turned over to the local or provincial governments and continued as a general tax to finance the growing need for services at these jurisdictional levels.

The specific details for implementing this basic plan with its many possible modifications must be worked out by imaginative technicians who are completely familiar with the country and are able to judge the size of the administrative burden the government can successfully manage. While each country can profit by the experience of others, no two are likely to be so situated that they can follow exactly the same paths.

XI

OPPORTUNITIES FOR NONFISCAL APPLICATIONS

THIS STUDY has demonstrated that land taxes are among the most pliable and versatile of fiscal instruments. They are found in strikingly diverse country settings, ranging from highly developed to primitive agricultures and including almost every type of land tenure pattern; moreover, they accommodate important governmental functions other than raising revenue. By grafting regulatory or incentive provisions to their land taxes, many countries employ the taxes as vehicles for an assortment of economic and social objectives. Although the widespread resort to these provisions is not in itself an indication of their value as policy instruments, it at least proves the existence of numerous opportunities for nonfiscal applications in land taxation.

Because the principle of "taxation for nonfiscal purposes" is often the target of sharp criticism, particularly in the United States, it is necessary in introducing this subject to sound a note of caution. "To admit regulation to the family of tax policy considerations is not to give it blanket approval. It must be tested in each proposed use for its effectiveness in achieving the desired results, and for the undesirable effects it may have. Assuming that the nonfiscal goal is a desirable one, is taxation the most effective method of achieving it?" [1]

Many countries have learned that failure to employ discretion and restraint in nonfiscal applications of taxes can be a costly fiscal experience. Above all, governments should be alert to two insidious dangers: first, the usefulness of the taxes as fiscal in-

[1] Roy Blough, *The Federal Taxing Process* (New York, 1952), p. 422.

struments might be impaired, and, second, the equitableness of the taxes might be undermined. For example, if a policy of granting tax exemption to promote desirable activities of high social and economic priority were extended to cover a wide range of different activities, the result might be a serious erosion of the tax base, while shifting more of the tax load onto persons who may not have the capacity to carry it. With many classes of taxpayers eligible for the exemption, the intended incentive effects of the favorable tax treatment would probably be destroyed as well. In the past it has proved difficult for governments to resist special interest group pressures to broaden tax concessions which were originally pinpointed toward a few specific incentive needs.

Another point worth stressing is that the utility of tax incentives can be demonstrated less easily in agriculture than in industry, and less easily in underdeveloped than in developed countries. This is because of the tight grip of tradition on farmers in underdeveloped countries and of the comparative insensitivity of farmers to most types of financial stimuli. Moreover, it may be difficult to communicate to farmers, many of whom may be illiterate in the poorer countries, the advantages of special tax provisions and of how they might benefit from them.[2]

This final chapter will explore some possible nonfiscal uses of land taxes to further the agricultural development goals of the less developed countries.[3] Although the chapter will attempt to

[2] A striking example of the taxpayer's preference for simplified methods of tax computation, even though such methods do not give him the maximum tax advantage, is provided by the Swedish experience with alternative methods for calculating allowances for forest depletion. A study by M. B. Grainger (*Forest Taxation in Europe and New Zealand,* New Zealand Forest Service, Information Series, No. 11, 1950, p. 42) shows that 79 per cent of the cases followed the method which gave the lowest deduction for forest capital, whereas an alternative method which provided more than double this deduction was used in only 12 per cent of the cases reviewed.

[3] Walter W. Heller has compiled valuable information on the use of incentive devices in agricultural taxation in underdeveloped and more advanced economies. See his paper on "The Use of Agricultural Taxation for Incentive Purposes" in *Papers and Proceedings of the Conference on Agricultural Taxation and Economic Development* (Cambridge, 1954), pp. 222–244.

guide thinking in this area of tax policy by indicating those uses which seem to be especially advantageous, it will not go so far as to blueprint any proposals in detail. The latter must be done individually for each country in order to tailor each plan to the local institutional and economic environment.

Incentive Implications of Land Tax Structure

One reason for favoring certain types of land taxes over other types is that they contain structural features which produce desirable incentive pressures. Whenever the tax base is determined by the productive capacity of the land or by annual rental or capital value, the tax liability does not vary with actual output in any given period. Thus, the rewards to the individual cultivator or landlord for additional productive effort or investment are not likely to be reduced by the tax. By the same token, such a tax, being in effect a fixed charge against the land, can make it expensive for anyone to hold cultivable land idle or to use it below its capacity; thus, the liable taxpayer is subjected to financial pressure to realize at least a minimum income from his land. Those types of taxes which are assessed according to the annual harvest or the volume of marketings, on the other hand, do not embody similar incentive advantages.[4] Nor are the advantages found either in annual income taxes, which force the income recipient to share increments of income with the government, or in indirect taxes, which vary directly with sales or purchases.

To permit above-average returns on individual farms to go tax free involves some compromising of equity objectives, but this may not be a serious drawback in land taxation, which is not a refined instrument from an equity standpoint even under the best of circumstances. Recognizing the desirability of providing the maximum incentive for farmers to adopt better techniques of cultivation, the preceding chapter recommended that the land

[4] See Chapter VIII, pp. 142–146.

tax yield should be made more flexible by across-the-board adjustments in accordance with regional price and production changes, rather than by individual adjustments for each taxpayer. Under the suggested plan, the marginal tax rate would be zero with respect to the individual farmer, but it would be positive with respect to farmers in the aggregate.

While an impersonal land tax base serves a nonfiscal purpose by eliminating a possible tax obstacle to increased production, probably its immediate justification can be found in administrative considerations. There are many nonfiscal applications, however, which can be recommended expressly for their potential value as incentive measures. In their basic approach, these applications provide either for tax penalties on undesirable activities or for tax concessions to desirable ones. Some of the more important ones are examined below.

Special Incentive Applications

In the following discussion the proposals for incentive applications of land taxes are classified broadly according to these principal objectives: (1) to increase production, (2) to redirect production, and (3) to penalize uneconomic land use. It should be recognized, however, that the scope for incentive applications extends beyond these particular objectives and may include, for example, influencing land tenure arrangements or favoring native as against foreign producers. Indeed, there is no limit to the number of tax incentive devices which might conceivably be applied to promote governmental policies. However, one should not lose sight of the fact that only a few have been conspicuously successful in operation and that many possible devices would clash sharply with equity objectives.

Although nonfiscal objectives of the type considered below may be aided or thwarted by basic structural features of the taxes, under favorable conditions these objectives can be furthered by adding special provisions which soften the tax impact in selected areas or provide stronger tax inducements. Nevertheless, any claims of their more enthusiastic supporters that some of these incentive arrangements are panaceas obviously should be rejected, since such claims are totally misleading as to what might realistically be expected.

To Increase Production

A common land tax provision intended to encourage larger agricultural output is the exemption of newly reclaimed land from taxation for a specified number of years. Such an exemption has obvious appeal because of its administrative simplicity and its direct effect in removing taxation as a factor reducing the potential rewards from land improvement activities such as drainage and clearance.

The recurrent proposal to exclude the value of buildings from the assessment base for real estate taxes places a similar emphasis upon possible incentive effects. The most common purpose of such an exclusion, however, is to give added encouragement to residential building, with the expectation that a larger supply of housing would yield important social benefits.[5] From this standpoint the proposal is more applicable to urban than to farm land, since the value of buildings is greater relative to land value in cities than in agricultural regions.[6] Nevertheless, there would seem to be many opportunities for employing the exemption principle to encourage increased productive investment in farm

[5] See Jens P. Jensen, "Exemption of Improvements," *Tax Exemption* (Tax Policy League, New York, 1939), pp. 206–231.

[6] Buildings and sometimes house sites are excluded from the tax base in most countries having land taxes that are assessed according to the productive capacity of the land. In the United States, the states that exempt buildings from the property tax base are in some of the *least* urban areas. North Dakota, for example, has a clear-cut exemption of buildings from property tax assessment; this was enacted in the 1930's as a depression measure, as a form of tax relief for farmers. Among European countries, Denmark has one of the most developed (and complex) systems of differential taxation of land and buildings. See E. B. Wistrich, "Local Revenue in Eleven Other Countries," Royal Institute of Public Administration, 1956, mimeographed, pp. 15, 17.

structures and agricultural land improvements of various sorts.[7] Most of the desired encouragement can probably be obtained by limiting the exemption to a specified number of years rather than having it continue indefinitely.[8]

Apart from structures and land reclamation, other land improvements such as irrigation, grading, fencing, and investment in soil conservation might be granted tax exemption for limited periods up to, say, five years. It would seem advisable to hold the exemption to a reasonably short duration, for otherwise any tax increases needed to compensate for the narrowing of the tax base could conceivably affect production adversely and more than offset the stimulating effect of the exemption. The exemption should of course be restricted to private investment, since it would serve no purpose as an inducement to government investment in agricultural development. Increases in the productive capacity of land resulting from government investment should be included in the tax base.

Exemptions from land taxes might also serve to increase production in various other ways; for example, by encouraging certain types of enterprises, such as co-operatives, and even by attracting additional foreign investment in agriculture. Many states in Mexico, for instance, impose lower rates on communal property than on private holdings; and in Chile, "immigration companies" which obtain at least 40 per cent of their capital from

[7] In 1956 Jamaica replaced its old land tax with a new tax based on unimproved land value, in the expectation that the new basis would provide an incentive to land improvements. Significantly, some students of land taxation in Jamaica are critical of the change. See J. R. and U. K. Hicks, *Report on Finance and Taxation in Jamaica* (Kingston: Government Printer, 1955), pp. 133–143; and D. J. Morgan, "Land Valuation and Land Taxation in Jamaica," *Public Finance,* no. 3 (1957), pp. 232–238. The methods followed in Australia, New Zealand, and a number of other countries which tax unimproved land value separately from the value of improvements are described in Ernest Long, "The Taxation of Land Values," A Paper Submitted to the 54th Annual Conference of the Institute of Municipal Treasurers and Acountants, Edinburgh, June 1939 (reprinted September 1946). Long's description is drawn from a study by A. W. Masden, "Land Value Taxation in Practice."

[8] See Hicks, pp. 136–143.

foreign sources are relieved of real estate taxes for five years.

The efficacy of exemptions as incentive measures is, of course, partly dependent upon the level of land taxation; where the level is low, as in much of Latin America, the exemption would count for little. Furthermore, like all incentive proposals exemptions are unlikely to bring results unless a sufficiently strong profit motive exists among farmers and unless taxpayers understand how the special provisions operate. To be sure, these conditions need not be satisfied if the exemptions are intended merely to lighten the tax load on certain groups, without necessarily influencing their economic behavior.

Occasional proposals have been advanced for more refined tax incentive devices to encourage increased agricultural production. One such proposal which has attracted wide attention, although it does not seem to have been considered seriously for enactment, was made by an International Bank mission to Colombia in 1950.[9] According to the mission's findings, "probably the most important single factor making for low productivity in agriculture in Colombia is the uneconomic and paradoxical use of land." [10] The following summary of the mission's recommendation on land taxation is taken from a United Nations publication:

> In order to achieve maximum utilization of land, the Mission recommends a system of taxation which is to penalize under-utilization of good land.
>
> The first step would be to revalue for land tax purposes the best farm lands of the country. The basic rate of 4 pesos per thousand enacted in 1948 would be increased progressively as the net income from the land falls below a certain percentage return on the current market value of the land as determined by the Geographical and Cadastral Institute. Different norms of rates of return would be established for the different categories of land. The basic tax rate would only apply to land producing the standard rate of return. Land undergoing reforestation or planted in cacao or palm nut trees would be exempted from the progressive rates.

[9] *The Basis of a Development Program for Colombia,* Report of a Mission Sponsored by the International Bank for Reconstruction and Development (Washington, 1950), pp. 384–387.

[10] *Ibid.*, p. 383.

It is expected that, in addition to providing a direct stimulus to more intensive farming, the proposed system would also operate to depress inflated land values and thus put better land within the reach of poorer farmers.[11]

It is difficult to believe that many underdeveloped countries possess the administrative and technical skills needed to operate successfully an elaborate tax scheme of this nature. Moreover, there is no evidence to suggest that the response of farmers to the proposed schedule of tax differentials would be sufficient, from the standpoint of the stimulus given to better land utilization, to justify its cost. The available information indicates, however, that Colombia, as well as other Latin American countries, can do much more than at present to encourage improved land use simply by revising obsolete assessments and increasing the tax rates, and also by imposing special taxes on cultivable land that is held idle.[12]

To Redirect Production

The opportunities for land tax arrangements which penalize or subsidize particular crops or agricultural activities would seem to be practically limitless.[13] Some systems of weighting the different kinds of farm output by unit prices or equivalency ratios is unavoidable under most types of land taxes, and it would be an easy matter to adjust the weighting in order to create the desired

[11] *Taxes and Fiscal Policy in Underdeveloped Countries*, United Nations Technical Assistance Administration (New York, 1954), pp. 60–61.

[12] In an attempt to bring assessed values close to market values, the government of Guatemala limits mortgage loans to 50 per cent of the assessed value of the property. The International Bank Mission to Nicaragua recommended basing credit appraisals on property values declared for tax purposes and also giving any person or government unit the right to bid for a property at twice the declared values. See *Taxes and Fiscal Policy in Underdeveloped Countries*, pp. 96–97.

[13] Heller cites the following examples: Cambodia's exemption of mulberry trees from the land tax, as a stimulus to silk culture; Chile's penalty tax on newly planted vineyards; and the favorable tax treatment in some Brazilian states for land planted to specified crops or used for grazing high-grade livestock (p. 227). There are also many examples of countries employing export and import duties, multiple exchange rates, and state marketing board operations to influence the pattern of production.

incentive inducements. Moreover, it is ordinarily necessary to rely upon different methods of assessment and different rates for, say, orchard fruits, garden vegetables, staple grains, nonfood crops, and livestock products, and this necessity creates ready opportunities for tax discrimination in furtherance of national agricultural policy.

Unless the land tax differentials correspond with net income differentials, the taxes will not be "neutral" in their relative impact on different types of output; thus, they will probably contain built-in incentive pressures, by accident if not by design. Governments have the choice of (1) trying to assess the tax so that it is as nearly "neutral" as possible, which would probably be considered the most equitable policy; (2) planning the tax impact so that it varies in a manner consistent with development objectives; or (3) disregarding whatever discrimination is implicit in the tax assessments and being guided chiefly by administrative expediency. As a practical matter, some governments may have no alternative but the last, since administrative considerations are of overriding importance for them. As between choices one and two, it seems clear that neutrality should be the general aim of land tax policy, insofar as its impact on different types of output is concerned, and that discrimination in the interest of creating desirable directional pressures should be used sparingly and only for carefully selected purposes. Shifting from one crop to another may be severely limited by land and climatic differences, so that preferential treatment of particular groups of producers may not yield economic benefits to the country as a whole. To bring the desired production changes, the discrimination would probably need to involve relatively heavy tax penalties or concessions, for otherwise the incentive for producers to change their plans would be too weak to overcome the forces favoring continuance of the status quo. In fact, in those countries where a strong profit motive is noticeably lacking in the agricultural population, any attempt to redirect production through tax pressure alone would seem futile. Another objection to a policy of liberal tax differentials to redirect production is that it might be intolerable from an equity viewpoint.

Some samples may be given of types of production shifts which may be assisted by appropriately designed tax differentials. By granting more favorable tax treatment to commercial crops than to subsistence crops, a country with an expanding agricultural output might seek to encourage a relative shift to commercial agriculture in order to improve the economic position of the agricultural sector. Similarly, the land tax might favor important export products in an effort to gain additional foreign exchange, or it might provide concessions to domestic producers of crops normally imported, with the aim of making more foreign exchange available for other imports.

Though land taxes may be readily adapted to purposes such as those discussed above, there may nevertheless be more efficient instruments of government policy to use. Some countries may find advantages in relying upon other types of taxes or upon other techniques, such as outright subsidy payments or direct controls over production or distribution in order to achieve the desired results.

To Penalize Uneconomic Land Use

The practice of holding large tracts of good farm land idle, or of devoting fertile land to the grazing of cattle, is a pressing economic problem in several countries, notably in Latin America.[14] Wherever fertile land is scarce, this practice may depress the national standard of living; furthermore, withholding the better land from cultivation may also contribute to overuse and consequent erosion of soil on the slopes. This problem is usually encountered in conjunction with gross inequalities in the distribution of land ownership and with large-scale absentee ownership.

[14] For example, see discussion of this problem in *The Basis of a Development Program for Colombia*, pp. 383–384; also, Richard Goode, "Reconstruction of Foreign Tax Systems," *Proceedings of the Forty-fourth Annual Conference of the National Tax Association* (1951), p. 220.

Land may be purchased as a hedge against inflation or for reasons of prestige, and if it is taxed only lightly, the owner can afford to keep the land underutilized. Though this is a situation which should probably be attacked directly through land reform measures, various tax changes can help to bring it under control.

Provided the tax rate is not too low, a tax based on a realistic assessment of the land in its most productive use would provide a strong inducement to the owners to farm the land more intensively or to dispose of it to others who would do so. In many Latin American countries, however, intensive use of land taxes is blocked, sometimes for administrative reasons, but more often because of the opposition of politically powerful groups of large landowners.[15]

The following special tax measures have been found appropriate in a few countries: (1) a progressive land tax varying directly with the size of landholdings, so that it falls especially heavily on large estates; (2) a penalty tax on cultivable land that is held idle; (3) a special tax on land held by absentee owners; and (4) a substantial additional tax on speculative gains in land value. It is significant to note that recommendations along these specific lines are commonly found in the reports of tax missions. The International Bank Mission to Nicaragua in 1953 proposed a surtax to compel owners of idle land to lease or cultivate it. The missions to both Cuba and Colombia recommended taxing capital gains from the sale of unimproved land more heavily than gains from, say, the sale of business enterprises. It was also proposed to vary the capital gains rate inversely with the period of holding, in order to encourage long-term as against speculative investments.[16] Besides Australia and New Zealand, which have had considerable experience with taxes designed to discourage large holdings, especially by absentee landlords, progressive tax rates are applied in parts of Argentina and Brazil. In sections of Argentina absentee

[15] Goode, p. 220.

[16] See summaries of recommendations in *Taxes and Fiscal Policy in Underdeveloped Countries*, pp. 60, 65, and 96.

owners are also subject to additional taxation. Chile has a surcharge on noncultivated land, but it is believed to be seldom enforced.[17]

Special Assessments to Finance Development Projects

Finally, attention should be called to the possible use of special assessments, or betterment levies, to finance agricultural development projects. Special assessments can be defined as governmental charges imposed to cover part or all of the cost of specific public improvements which yield substantial benefits to the owners of the assessed properties. Although special assessments are largely an American institution, having their widest use in financing urban and suburban improvements, such as roads and sanitation and flood control projects, they may deserve a place in the financial plans of some less developed countries seeking noninflationary sources of funds. In the underdeveloped countries, "it seems quite clear that special localized benefits will greatly exceed costs in the case of many projects in the general fields of irrigation, drainage, and rural highway transportation." [18]

Special assessments can be endorsed on equity grounds, because they are paid only by owners of properties which appreciate in value as a result of localized benefits associated with the improvement being financed. Conversely, it might be considered inequitable to finance out of general revenue a project which would benefit primarily a limited group of property owners. Special assessments can also be recommended from the standpoint of economic policy, because they do not interfere with production incentives.

Because landowners may be presumed not to have the ready

[17] United Nations Department of Economic Affairs, "Structure and Taxation of Agriculture in Chile," *Conference on Agricultural Taxation*, p. 346.

[18] E. R. Schlesinger, "The Use of Special Assessments to Finance Development Projects," International Bank for Reconstruction and Development (mimeographed, July 15, 1953), p. 5.

cash, the capital cost of the project cannot be realized in a lump sum upon completion of the project. Thus, the initial financing must be met through other revenue or loans, with the outlay being recovered as the collections based upon the special assessment are received. In order to avoid forced land sales, it may be desirable to delay the collections until the project actually yields higher income to the landowners or cultivators. Not only is it necessary to apportion the assessment so that no one is required to pay more than the benefits he receives, but it is also necessary to allow for the effect of raising land valuations for tax purposes once the improvement is completed. The objective of the assessment should be to tax away a substantially higher proportion of the added benefit than would be taxed under the regular land tax; this is an appropriate objective because the added benefit is attributable to government rather than private investment. Since most projects will yield general as well as localized benefits, it is usually not necessary that the total cost be recovered through special assessments.

The comparatively exacting administrative requirements of special assessments, however, may be a formidable obstacle to their use in some countries. In general, the countries and regions having the most efficient land taxes are likely to be the ones best able to take advantage of this financing method. In order to avoid injustices and adverse economic effects, satisfactory methods must be found for identifying the boundaries of the benefiting area and for apportioning the assessment equitably among the individual properties within the area. These steps may require engineering cost data and reasonably accurate land value appraisals that may not be readily obtainable. To warrant collecting such data, the special localized benefits of the project should be large relative to the total cost of the project.

The possibility of financing certain development projects with the aid of special assessments may provide an important inducement to undertake such projects especially when the government is under budgetary pressure. To some extent, therefore, special assessments are liable to the same criticism levied against earmarking of tax revenues, because the availability of financing through special assessments may lead to government investment which would deprive higher priority projects of needed resources. On the other hand, the development plans of many countries probably include a number of highly essential projects which lend themselves to assessment financing and can be undertaken without intensifying inflationary pressures.

Conclusions

The special land tax applications examined in this chapter should be viewed as possible appendages to the basic plan set forth in the preceding chapter. This sequence of topics is intended to emphasize the importance of a country's giving priority to needed reform in the land tax proper and not permitting its attention to be diverted from this need to proposals for special applications which, while sometimes offering large potential benefits, are really not the primary concern of tax policy.

The scope of possible nonfiscal applications is exceedingly broad and the policy issues raised are exceedingly complex. To build a strong case in their favor one must demonstrate that the objectives sought are proper, that the tax instrument is an appropriate one to use, that any expected revenue loss can be afforded, that the economic setting is suitable, that serious conflicts with equity considerations can be avoided, that the government's administrative machinery can carry the added load, and that their adoption will not establish precedents which will force the government to extend favorable tax treatment to more and more groups. This is a formidable list of preconditions, none of which can be ignored without risking unfortunate consequences. Nevertheless, the list is not impossible to satisfy. In fact, there is a body of tested experience which proves the existence of favorable opportunities for limited use of these measures in some countries.

INDEX

Bei Fragen zur Produktsicherheit wenden Sie sich bitte an:
If you have any questions regarding product safety,
please contact:

Walter de Gruyter GmbH
Genthiner Straße 13
10785 Berlin
productsafety@degruyterbrill.com